Wisterias

Wisterias

A COMPREHENSIVE GUIDE

Peter Valder

TIMBER PRESS
Portland, Oregon

For Allan

Pront cover: *Wisteria floribunda* 'Honbeni'
Back cover: *Wisteria floribunda* 'Kuchibeni' in autumn
Title pages: *Wisteria floribunda* 'Macrobotrys' framing a garden view
Below: *Wisteria sinensis* growing wild in Zhejiang

First published in North America in 1995 by
Timber Press, Inc.
133 S. W. Second Ave, Suite 450
Portland Oregon 97204 USA

Text and photographs © Peter Valder 1995

ISBN 0 88192 318 4

Editor: James Young
Designer: Stan Lamond, Lamond Art & Design
Printer: Kyodo Printing Co., Ltd, Singapore

Contents

Preface

Some plants repeatedly capture the imagination of gardeners and those otherwise interested in plants. Books are written about them, societies formed, shows held, breeding programmes initiated and expeditions sent to observe and collect species in the wild. One only has to think of camellias, irises, lilies, magnolias, rhododendrons and roses, to name a few.

As a gardener I have been through enthusiasms for all of these and many more, including the wisterias, which have brought me as much pleasure and interest as any cultivated plants I have encountered. So, after half a century of observation and forty years of collecting and growing them, I have been moved to record much of what I have learned.

In a world in which the annual production of gardening books, most of which have nothing new to tell us, must surely be capable of causing the collapse of every coffee table in existence, you might well ask why I have bothered. Well, as far as I know, no one has previously written a book on the subject in any European language. Also, a great deal of misinformation has been perpetuated in the existing literature and the nomenclature is in disarray. Thus I hope that what I have recorded here will not only save intending wisteria growers much time, annoyance and expense, but that it will also encourage others to take an interest in these strikingly handsome plants.

While I have made the acquaintance of several species and over forty cultivars, I have not seen all those known to exist. However the point has been reached where there is a lot that can be said and it seemed wise not to put it off any longer. Perhaps I, or someone else, may have the

Opposite   Japanese wisterias at Nooroo, Mount Wilson, NSW

opportunity of providing additions and amendments later on.

Some of the information is of a botanical or otherwise technical nature and may not be of interest to everyone. However I hope that I have arranged it in a manner that will enable those readers to avoid the sections that are not of interest to them. The book includes material from many previously published sources, which are acknowledged in the text as 'Wilson (1916)' or '(Wilson 1916)' and suchlike, according to circumstance. Those wishing to see a full reference may do so by consulting the list of references arranged alphabetically beginning on page 154.

As is usual with all such enterprises as this, a great many people have been of enormous help in offering advice, making plants available for inspection and providing information. Without the assistance, encouragement and support of my late father, my mother and Gerry and Jean Lenihan I would never have been able to grow and observe as many species and cultivars. And if it were not for the support and assistance of Allan McNeish, who got me started with word-processing, accompanied me on wisteria ventures round the world, pruned our forty wisterias year after year and exhibited astonishing patience, this book could never have appeared.

I am particularly indebted, too, to Trevor Davies of Auckland for sharing his enthusiasm for and extensive knowledge of wisterias with me, for taking me to see wisterias in New Zealand, for giving me plants, for coming to see my family's collection in Australia and for being a tireless correspondent. To his wife, Mary, I also extend my thanks.

In Australia I should also particularly like to thank Geoff Breen, Simon Goodwin, Anna Hallett, Ian Innes, David Mackay, Ian McClellan and Dr Peter Weston, all of the Royal Botanic Gardens, Sydney, for their help in various ways; Richard Clough for frequent advice and for providing references; Dr Laurie Jessup for looking at specimens for me while Australian Botanical Liaison Officer at Kew; Rie Shiraishi for her assistance with Japanese translations; Jackie Menzies and Ann Macarthur of the Art Gallery of New South Wales for arranging for me to view Japanese works of art; Edwina Jans of the Historic Houses Trust of New South Wales for providing information about Alexander Macleay; Michael Priest of New South Wales Agriculture for information on wisteria diseases; Gillean Dunk for advice about getting started; Gilbert Teague for arranging to have the book published; and Stan Lamond and James Young for getting it into shape. My thanks go too to the staff of the University of Sydney Library, the library of the Royal Botanic Gardens, Sydney, and the State Library of New South Wales for their assistance.

In China, Liu Gang and Yang Wei-hong of the Shanghai Botanic Garden showed me wisterias there and kindly took me to see the ancient vine at Zi Teng Peng Zeng. In Beijing, Professor Zhang Zhiming arranged for me to be received at the Beijing Botanical Garden by Meng Rengong and Professor Dong Bahua. Professor Dong told me where to find wisterias in and around Beijing and Mr Meng provided much useful information as well as seeds of the Beijing form of *W. sinensis*. My thanks go to all these people.

In Japan, Hideo Suzuki was most kind in giving advice and coming with me to visit Shigeru Kawarada, whose unrivalled knowledge of Japanese wisterias he so generously shared with me. I am particularly grateful, too, to Professor Kenichi Arisumi for leading me to references and descriptions of wisterias in the Japanese horticultural literature, to Junzo Sawa for help with translations, and to Yuri Kurashige for sending me seeds of *W. brachybotrys* collected in the wild.

Various people in England have been most

supportive. My special thanks go to Chris Brickell and Dr Alan Leslie for their advice about nomenclature, Peter Elliman of Cannington College for arranging for me to examine the National Wisteria Collection, Mrs John Gaggini for allowing me to look at plants at the Mears Ashby Nursery, Jonathon Nettleton of Nettleton's Nursery for descriptions of cultivars and David Sayers for advice about where to find wisterias in South Korea. I am also most grateful to the staff of the libraries at the Royal Botanic Gardens, Kew, and the Royal Horticultural Society for their help. My thanks go to the Director of the Royal Botanic Gardens, Kew, for providing me with the opportunity to examine the wisteria specimens in the herbarium.

And in Switzerland Fay and Alex Knecht of Quartino were most kind in taking me to Otto Eisenhut's nursery at San Nazzaro and to the garden of Sir Peter Smithers at Vico Morcote.

In the United States the staff of the libraries of the New York Botanical Garden, the Massachusetts Horticultural Society and the Pennsylvania Horticultural Society were all most welcoming, as were the staff of the Gray Herbarium, Harvard University, who arranged for me to examine specimens there. To Dr Jeff Doyle of the Liberty Hyde Bailey Hortorium, Dr Matt Lavin of Montana State University and Professor Aaron Liston of Oregon State University, I am indebted for guiding me towards an understanding of the modern approach to legume taxonomy. Also most helpful were Rick Darke and Robert Herald at Longwood Gardens, Pennsylvania, Dr Tom Delendick at the Brooklyn Botanic Garden, Gary Koller at the Arnold Arboretum and Jack Potter at the Scott Arboretum of Swarthmore College, all of whom showed me the respective wisteria collections. And Jean Lane of Portola Valley, California, was most kind in taking me to Filoli, where there is another extensive collection.

For detailed information about wisteria cultivars in North America I am indebted to Mark Andrews of the Greenleaf Nursery Company, Ken Durio of the Louisiana Nursery, John Elsley of Wayside Gardens, William Flemer III of the Princeton Nurseries, Robert Ludekens of the L. E. Cooke Company, Robert McCartney of Woodlanders, Professor J. C. Raulston of North Carolina State University, Audrey Teasedale of the Monrovia Nursery Company and David Thompson of the Foxborough Nursery.

For providing photographs my thanks go to the Bibliothèque Nationale de France (figure 4.9), Janet Evans of the Pennsylvania Horticultural Society (figure 5.10), Karen Kane of the Arnold Arboretum, who arranged for the printing of Ernest Wilson's negatives (figures 5.4, 5.7, 5.40), the Lindley Library of the Royal Horticultural Society (figure 4.2), Dr Peter McGee (figure 2.5), the Monrovia Nursery Company (figure 6.5) and the Tokyo National Museum (figure 5.3). Permission to reproduce illustrations from *The Flowers and Gardens of Japan* (figure 5.8), *The Garden Flowers of China* (figure 4.10) and *Gardens of China* (figures 4.12, 4.14 and 4.16) was sought from A. & C. Black (Publishers) Ltd and John Wiley & Sons, Inc. All other photographs are my own. The black and white line drawings are by David Mackay.

CHAPTER 1

Wisteria or Wistaria?

With the magic of the expanding inflorescence buds in spring, the form, colour, scent and arrangement of the flowers, the elegant disposition of the foliage, the fascinating pendulous seed pods, the autumn colour of most kinds and, particularly in winter, the wonderful gnarled trunks and twisted branches of old vines, wisterias have few competitors when it comes to garden ornament.

One of my earliest horticultural memories is of an old lattice summer-house collapsing under the weight of a plant of the Chinese Wisteria, *Wisteria sinensis*. This grew in the garden of a house in which, at the age of four, I attended a small kindergarten. A picture of the mass of scented flowers has remained with me ever since. And enveloping the tankstand of another house nearby was a different wisteria, of which in 1935 my father was given a sucker. This plant we were told was Japanese rather than Chinese and came to us with the intriguing name 'Multijuga'.

My father planted it to grow over a pergola he built for it outside our back door. Within a year of two it began producing its long racemes, hanging down to form a curtain of scented flowers, buzzing with bees. The pergola was progressively enlarged to accommodate it and it has continued to provide annually one of the great sights of the garden (pages 2–3 and figure 5.28). Often its racemes are a metre long and on one occasion in its youth we measured some 1.3 m in length. So even as a child it became clear to me that wisterias were plants to be reckoned with.

Figure 1.1   Racemes of *Wisteria sinensis*

From the same garden my father later obtained 'Multijuga Alba' and a pale pink one, 'Carnea'. And growing by the kitchen door of the house where I went to the kindergarten was another that produced, rather sparingly, double flowers of deep violet. So we asked for and were given a piece of that too, though the owner did not know its name.

For some reason my father did not bother with *W. sinensis* until after World War II, when both the mauve and white forms arrived, as did 'Rosea', a deeper pink form of the Japanese Wisteria, which a nursery nearby had imported from Holland. We now had seven sorts and the beginnings of nomenclatural confusion.

About this time I began reading everything I could find about wisterias in the expectation that there might be more kinds. I soon came across the excellent article by Donald Wyman in *Arnoldia* published in June 1949 (Wyman 1949), an expanded version of which appeared in the *American Nurseryman* in 1961 (Wyman 1961). These articles were based on his experiences with the extensive collection at the Arnold Arboretum, which comprised some thirty species and cultivars.

As a result of reading these articles and others, I was made aware of the existence of several species and a considerable number of named cultivars. Early in 1963 I obtained from the J. Clarke Nursery Company of San Jose, California, *W. floribunda* cultivars named 'Geisha', 'Issai', 'Longissima', 'Longissima Alba' and 'Royal Purple', as well as white and mauve forms of what in their catalogue was called *W. venusta*. In addition the Arnold Arboretum sent me scions of several other cultivars. All these survived the rigours of treatment by the quarantine service and were established in containers. We also had the catalogue of the Chugai Nursery Company near Kobe for 1959–60, in which were listed eleven wisterias. Although their names were different, with the exception of *W. japonica* they seemed from their descriptions to be no different from plants we already had, so we took the matter no further.

As it was we had not come up with an answer as to how all these vigorous climbers could be accommodated in our modest garden. But before long the problem was solved by what insurance companies call an Act of God.

When we had given up playing tennis we had converted our tennis court into a shadehouse, supporting a slatted roof with twenty-eight uprights in addition to those making up the original boundary fence. In July 1965 this, and much else in the garden, was demolished by an unusually heavy snowfall, the most severe anyone could remember. Assuming this would not happen again, the shadehouse was rebuilt, only to succumb to a similar catastrophe five years later.

This time we decided not to rebuild it but merely to replace the uprights and use them as supports for training the wisterias as standards. Thus, places were found for them and in turn shade was provided for the plants beneath. So began what has become a somewhat ideosyncratic wisteria garden (figure 1.2).

Since then I have continued to collect species and cultivars from China, Japan, North America and Europe, as well as from local sources. In most cases, whatever their names and descriptions, they have turned out to be the same as cultivars I had already acquired or even the seedling stock onto which at one time a named cultivar had been grafted. This, of course, is a common complaint of gardeners concerning almost any group of plants for which they have shown enthusiasm. Subsequently, I kept any new wisteria I obtained in our vegetable garden until it bloomed and demonstrated its identity before introducing it to the ornamental part of the garden—a long and

Figure 1.2   The wisteria garden at Nooroo, Mount Wilson, NSW

tedious business in the case of these plants but, alas, essential.

Because of this, and because gardeners often get annoyed with botanists for insisting on the use of names of Latin form, and, even worse, changing them from time to time, there follow a few words about the classification and nomenclature of plants. Those of you who already know about this, or do not wish to, may like to skip the rest of this chapter.

Classification and nomenclature

If we look at plants growing naturally in any particular place, we find that there are groups of individuals showing many common features. Such groups, recognisably distinct from others, are in general what are called species. It has been found convenient to group those species with most features in common into more inclusive groups called genera (singular 'genus'). Genera in turn are grouped into families and so on. Thus a hierarchical system of classification is built up.

Plants, of course, are unaware that humans are anxious to name and classify them, putting them into a number of nice distinct compartments. Quite often a plant exhibits characteristics which make it hard for us to decide which compartment to put it in. Then we have to make up our minds where it fits most happily or make a new compartment for it. And so we get the 'lumpers' and 'splitters' you may have heard about. The best advice for gardeners about all this is to remain calm and keep an open mind. In these days of computers and DNA technology we are likely to be confronted with a great deal more change.

It must be remembered that the purpose of names is to avoid the need for the repeated use of cumbersome descriptive phrases and to act as vehicles of communication. To be effective they must be unambiguous and universal. Common names of plants do not meet these conditions. Quite apart from the multiplicity of languages, many using different alphabets, even within one language a single name may be applied to several different plants, or one species may be known by more than one common name.

For these reasons common names are quite unsatisfactory for use in botanical nomenclature, where every effort is made to avoid such defects. For this reason a set of rules called the *International Code of Botanical Nomenclature* has been drawn up (Greuter et al. 1988). While these rules do not have any status in international law, botanists in general observe their provisions.

To be universal, scientific names must be written in the one alphabet and the one language. The Code requires that all scientific names be Latin in form and conform to the rules of Latin grammar. Thus, these names are Latin or treated as if they are, whatever their derivation.

The names of species consist of two terms and are therefore called 'binomial'. The name of a species consists of the name of the genus in which it has been placed followed by a 'specific epithet' which is peculiar to the species, for example *Rosa canina,* the dog rose or common briar. The genus to which the species belongs is *Rosa*, and the specific epithet is *canina.* This system of naming goes back to Linnaeus's *Species Plantarum* of 1753.

Now, if you haven't gone off to do something else by this, there are some other matters that need mentioning. In botanical literature it is the convention that the first time the name of a species is used, it is followed by one or more personal names, sometimes abbreviated, for example *Rosa canina* L. Here the 'L.' stands for

Linnaeus. And this means that the name was first published by Linnaeus. Linnaeus is thus the author of the name and the 'L.' is known as an authority citation. The authority citation is not part of the scientific name but is essentially an abbreviated reference that adds to nomenclatural precision. This is particularly useful where the same name has been used for different species or different names for the one species, before the matter has been sorted out.

In case not everyone is clear about all this, a botanical name follows in the form of a diagram, from which it should be clear that the name of the species is made up of the name of the genus plus the specific epithet.

Name of Species

It is the convention for the generic name and the specific epithet to be printed in italics, or at least in a typeface different from that used in the general text. If handwritten or typed it is usual for them to be underlined. The name of the genus should have a capital initial letter and that of the specific epithet a small one. Even when the specific epithet is derived from a proper noun or a person's name it is usual to use a small initial letter.

The second term of the binomial has no standing by itself and cannot be used alone to refer to any plant. The word *canina,* for instance, simply means 'pertaining to dogs' and by itself cannot accurately refer to any particular kind of plant.

Once the full name of a species has been cited in a text, the generic name is often abbreviated to its initial letter in subsequent citations, if this can be done without causing ambiguity or doubt. For example, we can now write *R. canina,* as the full name has already been mentioned and no ambiguity would ensue.

The aim of the Code is for every species to have one valid, universally recognisable name. The rules state that the first validly published name shall have priority. Thus, where a species has been given more than one name, it is the one first validly published which stands. Sometimes, however, the name by which a plant is universally known is discovered not to be the name it was first validly given. In such cases the botanists sometimes weaken, thank goodness, and, at one of the international botanical congresses held every few years, agree to conserve the well-known name. When they don't, you must try to understand that it is all well-intentioned and designed to reduce confusion even if, like most change, it takes a little getting used to.

Some botanists and gardeners get very pedantic about pronunciation, though it is debatable that anyone really knows how the Romans pronounced Latin and whether they all pronounced it the same way. It also seems likely that, as with other languages, there were changes over the centuries. It is my view that, as with all foreign words, it is best not to fuss. Botanical Latin is not real Latin anyway, since plant names are frequently based on words from a wide variety of ancient and modern sources. The Romans didn't have a 'j', 'u' or 'w' and they certainly hadn't heard of *Wisteria* or *Eschscholzia* for that matter. If you look carefully at any botanical name and pronounce all the syllables without thinking much about it, you will probably make a pretty good job of it anyway and get most of the accents where the purists say they should go. And as long as whoever you are talking to knows what you mean, then all is well.

Well now, let us see how all this affects wisterias. A broader classification for plants, above that of genus, is family. Plants are grouped into

families according to broad similarities. The genus *Wisteria* is placed in the legume family, which includes, among other things, all the plants with pea-shaped flowers and which typically produce fruits known as legumes. Pea pods, for instance, are legumes. Currently botanists consider *Wisteria* to belong to that group of legumes known as the tribe Millettieae (Geesink 1984). (A tribe is a kind of subcategory of a family.) The genus is the only entirely temperate representative of the tribe, the others being largely tropical. However it is considered to fit most conveniently here on account of its members exhibiting many characteristics in common with the other genera included, notably in being woody vines with pinnate leaves and hypogeal germination. On the other hand DNA analysis indicates that *Wisteria* has characteristics suggesting affiliation with herbaceous genera in other tribes (Lavin, Doyle & Palmer 1990; Liston 1994), so the problem of its relationships is far from resolved.

The genus, as presently understood, consists of perhaps no more than eight species, possibly only five. Two of these are native to eastern North America and the remainder to eastern Asia. The genus is one of a number, *Magnolia, Liriodendron, Liquidambar* and *Chionanthus* for example, which have this interesting distribution, the existing species being separated by western North America and the Pacific Ocean. The Asian species are very similar to one another as are the American ones, and the determination of the actual number of distinct species awaits a detailed study of the genus both in the wild and in the laboratory. Added to this is the complication that at least one author (Stritch 1984) considers the Asian species to be sufficiently distinct to warrant them being placed in a separate genus of their own, *Rehsonia*. However, until further investigations are carried out it seems wise to leave them in *Wisteria*.

Another source of confusion is that *Millettia*

japonica is also sometimes considered to belong to *Wisteria*. It occurs in Japan, has a similar habit and has recently been shown to have the same DNA peculiarity as *Wisteria* (Liston 1994). Even so it differs in a number of ways from both *Millettia* and *Wisteria*. According to Geesink (1984), it is better referred to the recently resurrected genus *Callerya*, at least for the time being, on account of its generally paniculate inflorescence, often combined with axillary racemes, and the dehiscent pods. However, in her recent revision of the genus *Callerya,* Schot (1994) has not included it among the species she considers to belong here. So rather than cause further confusion I shall continue to call this plant *M. japonica* for the present.

Wisterias have been around for a long time, a fossil species, *W. falax,* dating from the Miocene Period (somewhere between 7 000 000 and 26 000 000 years ago), having been found in Shandong, China (Guo & Zhou 1992). In the countries where they now occur naturally, they have been known and given names for hundreds, perhaps thousands, of years. They came to European notice, however, only relatively recently.

Undoubtedly as a result of the sensible attitudes of the Chinese and Japanese in keeping foreigners at bay, the first wisteria to become known in Europe came from America. This was introduced from Carolina about 1724 and given the name *Glycine frutescens* by Linnaeus in his *Species Plantarum* of 1753. It had been described earlier and given other names but the *Species Plantarum* has been agreed to be the starting point for botanical nomenclature.

Quite independently the Anglo-American botanist Thomas Nuttall (1818) named the plant *Wisteria speciosa* in his book *The Genera of North American Plants*. Of the name *Wisteria* Nuttall recorded that it was in memory of Caspar Wistar, late Professor of Anatomy at the University of

Pennsylvania. As a result people often write or say *Wistaria* instead of *Wisteria* though the latter spelling is the one Nuttall published. Whether it was spelled that way by mistake or because he thought it sounded more like the way Wistar's name was pronounced we shall never know.

According to Elizabeth McClintock (1973), there is evidence that the son of Nuttall's coincidentally named friend Charles Wister Sr believed the genus was named for his father, so perhaps Nuttall had both Wistar and Wister in mind. We shall probably never know about that either.

Anyway Nuttall's original spelling was followed by most people and in 1906 was accepted as correct under the rules of the Code. So *Wisteria* it is, whatever anyone might tell you.

But wait a minute, you say, had not Linnaeus named the same plant *Glycine frutescens* sixty-five years earlier? So surely this should be its correct name. Well the botanists decided that this plant did not fit comfortably in the genus *Glycine,* which now contains things such as the soybean, and that it should be in a separate genus for which *Wisteria* is the first validly published name. However, as it already had a validly published specific epithet, *frutescens*, this had priority over *speciosa*. The French botanist Jean Poiret (1823) published the corrected name, *Wisteria frutescens* (figure 1.3). Nevertheless the word 'glycine' has survived as the common name for wisteria in French. Mercifully, in English *Wisteria* is a genus that has the same common name as its botanical one, so far at any rate. And even should the Asian ones end up in a different genus, it is unlikely people would stop calling them wisterias.

As mentioned earlier, it is the convention that the first time a botanical name is cited, the name or names of the person or persons responsible for that name are included. This is done as the situation can and does arise where the one genus or species is given a different name by

Figure 1.3 *Wisteria frutescens*

different people, as has happened here. *Glycine frutescens* L. and *Wisteria speciosa* Nutt. were recognised to be the same by Poiret. Thus the name of this plant is properly written as *Wisteria frutescens* (L.) Poir. The 'L.' is placed in brackets to indicate the transfer of Linnaeus's plant from *Glycine* to *Wisteria* and the 'Poir.' indicates that this was done by Poiret. So the name cited above with its authority encapsulates its own history. Nuttall, incidentally does not miss out as he is the authority for the name *Wisteria*.

Those of you who have not given up by this will be relieved to know that the discussion about botanical classification and nomenclature ends here for the time being. Suffice it to say that at one time or another the various plants we now know as wisterias have been placed in the genera *Anonymos, Apios, Bradburya, Bradleya, Diplonyx, Dolichos, Glycine, Krauhnia, Millettia, Phaseoloides, Phaseolus, Rehsonia* and *Thyrsanthus*.

Finally a word about pronunciation. In the fourth edition of Bean's *Trees and Shrubs Hardy in the British Isles* it is suggested that we should pronounce it with a short 'e'. You, of course, may do as you wish but I am going to stay with wis-*teer*-e-a.

Naming cultivated plants

Let us look now at the naming of those variants of the wild species or plants of hybrid origin known as cultivated varieties or cultivars. On the whole it is best to avoid the use of the word 'variety' in this context as this name is used for a category in the hierarchy of botanical classification mentioned in the previous section. Thus there are both botanical and cultivated varieties. Confusion, then, is not likely to arise if we stick with the word 'cultivar', unattractive though it may be.

The naming of cultivars is another area where one almost always encounters disorder. But, again, there is now an *International Code of Nomenclature for Cultivated Plants* (Brickell et al. 1980) along the lines of the one for botanical nomenclature. Anyone thinking of naming a cultivar would be wise to consult it.

The gist of it is that, in most cases, the first properly published name is the correct one and that, after January 1959, you should not give cultivars Latin or confusing names and that the use of abbreviations is discouraged. Also discouraged is the use of titles or forms of address; that is, 'George Brown' is to be preferred rather than 'Sir George Brown' or 'Mr George Brown'. However, for some reason you are allowed to use 'Mrs', or its equivalent in other languages; that is 'Mrs George Brown' is permitted though surely 'Elizabeth Brown' would be preferable.

To distinguish them from botanical names, cultivar names should not be in italics or otherwise differentiated. Also, when immediately following a botanical or common name, a cultivar name should be distinguished by placing the abbreviation 'cv.' before it, or by the use of some typographic device, preferably by enclosing it within single quotation marks, that is, *W. sinensis* cv. Jako, *W. sinensis* 'Jako' or wisteria 'Jako'. It is usual for all words in the cultivar name with the exception of articles and prepositions to bear an initial capital. The code also recommends avoidance of an initial article, unless required by linguistic custom, and that new cultivar names should consist of one or two and no more than three words. Double quotation marks or the abbreviation 'var.' should not be used to distinguish cultivar names.

When a cultivar name precedes a common name it may be distinguished by a typographical device, preferably by enclosing it within single quotation marks, or it may be used without any particular distinction, provided there is no likelihood of confusion.

When a cultivar name is used apart from a botanical or common name it may be treated as in the preceding case or it may follow the abbreviation 'cv.' Perhaps the simplest course of action would be always to put cultivar names within single quotation marks.

It is also recommended that when a cultivar is named in another language the name not be translated. However, when such names are not in Roman script a transliteration is desirable.

In the case of wisterias this applies particularly to names written in Chinese or Japanese characters, to which the currently accepted systems of romanisation apply. Since these systems have not always been followed there is much variation in the literature in the way such names have been rendered in romanised form. The Japanese character for wisteria, for instance, is nowadays transliterated according to the Hepburn system as 'fuji', but in the past has appeared as 'fugi', 'fudsi', 'fudzi' and 'huzi'. There is similar variation in transliterations from Chinese, for which the Pinyin system is now used.

It must also be remembered that such transliterations are merely an attempt to reproduce the sound using the Roman alphabet. Further difficulties may arise because characters which are different and represent different things may be pronounced in the same way, and in many cases the same character may be pronounced in different ways with different meaning. And all the associations and nuances conjured up by the appearance of a character are lost to a foreigner reading the transliteration.

For many plants, including the wisterias, the names in Japanese nursery lists are often not really cultivar names at all but merely characters or romanisations meaning 'white wisteria' and suchlike. 'Murasaki Naga Fuji', for instance, sounds wonderful but merely means 'Purple Long Wisteria'. Even so, when a name such as this has been used consistently for a long time, it is probably wise to stay with it.

But among the wisterias, alas, the giving of different names to the one cultivar, together with a lack of information, has resulted in confusion similar to that pertaining to so many other groups of plants. To give but one example, and there are many others, the old Japanese cultivar *W. floribunda* 'Kuchibeni' (figure 1.4) has, in nursery catalogues, been listed variously as 'Carnea', 'Lipstick' and 'Peaches and Cream'. From time to time, cultivars are assigned to the wrong species as well. So the poor customers really need help.

In the absence of a registration authority for cultivar names in the genus *Wisteria*, it has been difficult to decide, in cases where a single cultivar has been given more than one name, which one to choose. The repeated use of names such as 'Alba' and 'Rosea' for cultivars of more than one species, together with the difficulties experienced by professional growers and others in distinguishing between the species, has led to much confusion. Thus it would seem to be unwise to

Figure 1.4   *Wisteria floribunda* 'Kuchibeni'

continue to use the same cultivar name more than once within the genus.

One of the aims of this book, then, is to make at least a preliminary attempt to sort things out. In making recommendations I have, of course, been guided by the Code. No doubt some of my views will be shown to be wrong, but it is hoped they will stimulate others to clarify the situation further.

C H A P T E R   2

Getting to Know the Plant

The life cycle

In order to understand, identify and successfully cultivate any plant, it is useful to know the names of its various parts and how it grows under natural circumstances. Let us begin with the seed.

The wisteria seed consists of a protective seed coat inside which is an embryonic plant in a dormant state. This embryonic plant is made up of a minute embryonic shoot (plumule) bearing two large, food-rich seed-leaves (cotyledons) and a minute embryonic root (radicle) (figure 2.2).

When provided with water and exposed to favourable temperatures, the seed swells, the embryo absorbing moisture and resuming development. The leaf-stalks (petioles) of the cotyledons elongate sufficiently to push the embryonic shoot and root clear of the seed coat. The embryonic root grows down into the soil and the embryonic shoot grows up into the air and light. It becomes green and develops leaves (figure 2.3), using the nutrients stored in the cotyledons, which remain within the seed coat. This type of germination, in which the cotyledons remain below the soil, is known as hypogeal.

These developments enable the young seedling to become independent, the root absorbing moisture and mineral nutrients from the soil and the shoot commencing photosynthesis, using light energy to convert carbon dioxide and water into the organic compounds needed for growth and development.

Figure 2.1   Seed pods of *Wisteria floribunda* 'Macrobotrys'

21

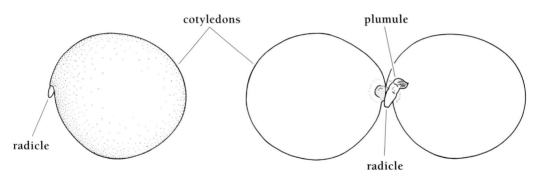

Figure 2.2 Wisteria seed: (*left*) with seed coat removed; (*right*)
with seed coat removed and cotyledons opened out

Wisterias produce compound leaves consisting of a leaf-stalk (petiole) and a central axis (rachis), bearing a number of leaflets in pairs plus a single one at the end (figure 2.4). This type of leaf is called pinnate. The stalks of the individual leaflets of compound leaves are known as petiolules. The leaves and other above ground parts may be hairless (glabrous) or covered, at least when young, with short soft hairs (pubescent). These hairs are usually less than 2 mm long, hence some magnification may be needed to observe them.

Although wisterias are woody plants their stems are weak and are not self-supporting. However, under natural conditions, they ensure that the leaves reach the light by climbing over rocks and/or other plants, securing and supporting themselves by twining. Like many vines they find conditions suitable for their development along riverbanks, on roadsides and on cliffs.

As the root system develops it becomes invaded by microorganisms. A bacterium, *Rhizobium* species, brings about the development of nodules (figure 2.5) in which atmospheric nitrogen is converted into compounds. Thus wisterias, like other legumes, are rendered independent of outside sources of nitrogen compounds in return for supplying the bacteria with the rest of the nutrients they require. Such an arrangement, which benefits both partners, is an example of symbiosis. It is well known that the use of effectively nodulated legumes in crop rotations maintains or improves the level of nitrogen compounds in the soil, a large industry having sprung up to provide the appropriate bacteria for inoculating the seed before planting. Thus, the need for adding nitrogenous fertilisers is avoided.

The roots of most legumes enter into a second symbiotic association, in this instance with a fungus. Such associations are called mycorrhizas and the type occurring in legumes is known as arbuscular, on account of the finely branched structures (arbuscules) which the fungus produces inside the cells of the host tissue (figure 2.6). The mycorrhizal fungus often produces swellings known as vesicles within the roots as well. The fungus obtains organic compounds from its host plant, which in return also benefits. The fungus extends further into the soil than the roots and hence is in a position to take up additional water, phosphorus and other minerals which are passed on to the plant. Thus mycorrhizal plants are able to grow more satisfactorily than non-mycorrhizal ones under natural conditions, as they have access to a better supply of nutrients and are also more drought-resistant. In addition to this there is evidence that plants which are mycorrhizal also have their disease-resistance enhanced.

Figure 2.3
Wisteria seed germinating

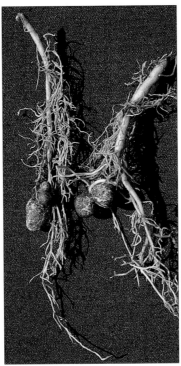

Figure 2.5
Wisteria root nodules

Figure 2.6
Arbuscular mycorrhiza.
Photomicrograph showing the
fungus (stained blue) within
the root tissue.

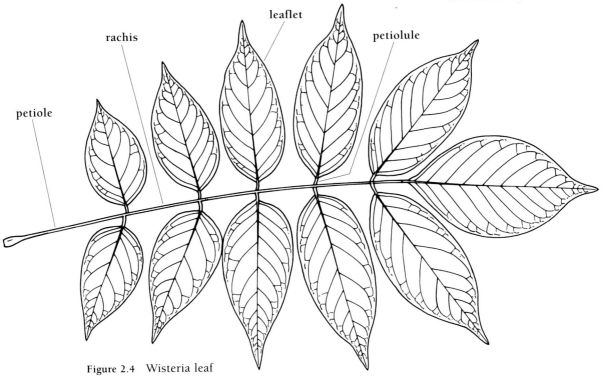

leaflet

rachis

petiolule

petiole

Figure 2.4   Wisteria leaf

Wisterias climb by twining either clockwise or anticlockwise and the direction of twining is one of the characters used in identifying the species. Determining the direction of twining is not as simple as it sounds and there is already some confusion in the literature about this. Those that twine clockwise when viewed from above are sometimes described as twining by climbing from right to left around the axis, though this is only on the side of the axis nearest the viewer (figure 2.7). They are actually climbing by twining spirally upwards around the axis by turning towards the right. The botanical term for this is 'dextrorse'. A glance at the illustration should make this confusing concept clear. Likewise those that twine in an anticlockwise direction when viewed from above are sometimes described as twining by climbing from left to right, though they are actually turning to the left (figure 2.8). The botanical term for this is 'sinistrorse'.

Figure 2.7
Clockwise
(dextrorse) twining
(*Wisteria floribunda*)

Figure 2.8
Anticlockwise
(sinistrorse) twining
(*Wisteria sinensis*)

Provided conditions are suitable, wisteria plants grow vigorously throughout the summer, ceasing as the days shorten and temperatures fall. In response to these stimuli they eventually become dormant and the leaves are shed. In the dormant state the plants are not damaged by temperatures below freezing, their cold-hardiness varying according to the species. At this stage it is usually possible to tell, with the Asiatic species at any rate, whether a plant will bloom the following season, as the buds which produce flowers in most cases are larger than those which produce only shoots (figures 2.9–2.12).

Following a period of winter dormancy, growth recommences in spring, when flowers are produced on the ends of short, leafy shoots, known as peduncles, on a structure known as a raceme. This has a central axis, the rachis, on which each flower is borne on a short stalk of its own, the pedicel (figure 2.13).

Each flower has a calyx with five lobes and five petals—a large, showy standard, two wings and a keel composed of two petals joined together along the distal parts of their lower edges (figure 2.14). Each petal has a slender attachment, the claw, and one or two projections called auricles. Within the boat-shaped keel are ten stamens, nine joined together and the uppermost one free. These surround the ovary, style and stigma.

In order for seeds to be produced, pollen must be placed on the stigma. This is the process called pollination. Pollination is usually performed by bees, which are attracted by the colour and scent of the flowers. The visiting bee, in search of pollen and the nectar secreted by the base of the stamens, is guided by the markings on the standard petal and alights on the wings (figure 2.15). As these and the keel have only slender attachments (figure 2.14), they are depressed by the weight of the bee, the abdomen of which makes contact with the upturned stamens and stigma, exposed

Figure 2.9   Inflorescence buds of
Wisteria sinensis

Figure 2.10   Inflorescence buds of *Wisteria brachybotrys* 'Shiro Kapitan'

Figure 2.11   Inflorescence buds of
Wisteria floribunda

Figure 2.12   Inflorescence buds of *Wisteria brachybotrys* 'Murasaki Kapitan'

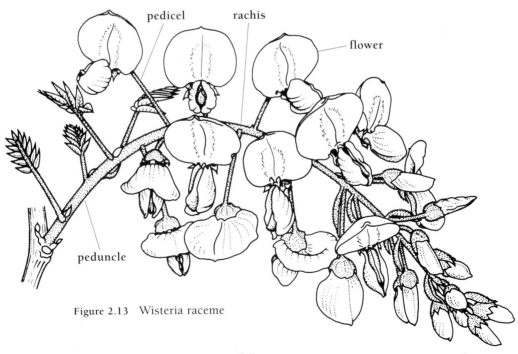

Figure 2.13   Wisteria raceme

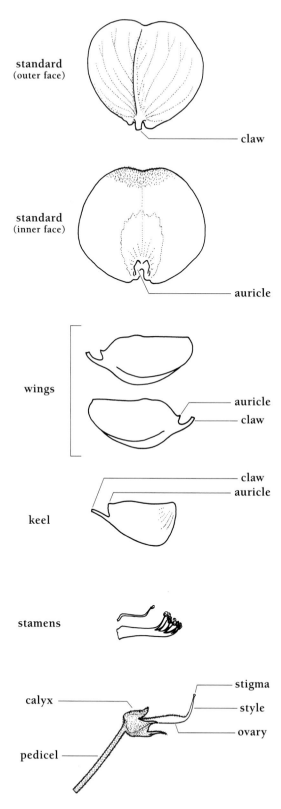

standard
(outer face)

claw

standard
(inner face)

auricle

wings

auricle
claw

claw
auricle

keel

stamens

stigma

calyx

style

ovary

pedicel

Figure 2.14   Structure of wisteria flower

by the depression of the keel. When the bee, now dusted with pollen, alights on the next flower, it deposits some of this pollen on the stigma.

In order for this to be possible the flower must be disposed with the standard petal uppermost. This involves no adjustment in the case of sweet peas or lupins where the raceme is upright. But in wisterias, where the raceme becomes pendulous, it is necessary for the pedicel of each flower to twist through 180 degrees as the flower approaches maturity in order for it to be suitably orientated for pollination. If you look closely at a wisteria raceme you will see buds at various stages of this twisting process (figure 2.16). This phenomenon has been recorded in the works of Japanese artists since early times (see figures 5.3 and 5.9 in chapter 5).

After pollen has been placed on the stigma it germinates, each grain sending a tube down the style into one of the ovules, as the embryonic seeds are called at this stage, where it fertilises the egg cell, which then develops into an embryonic plant of the next generation within the seed.

Each ovary contains a row of ovules, just like those in a pea pod, one or more of which may develop into a seed. As the seeds develop, the ovary surrounding them enlarges and develops, becoming the fruit, in this case a legume, though generally it is referred to less precisely as a pod (figure 2.1). This eventually opens by splitting down lines of dehiscence along each edge, the two halves separating to release the seeds.

Although wisteria racemes may have up to 170 flowers, it is unusual for more than one or two of these to produce a pod. The pods gradually become woody and remain on the plant long after the leaves have fallen. They then slowly dry out and on sunny days in late winter suddenly split open, making a loud cracking sound. The two halves twist as they separate (figure 2.17), flinging the seeds some distance, often a metre

Figure 2.15
Bee pollination of
wisteria flower

Figure 2.16
Flower buds turning through 180°,
bringing standard petal uppermost

Figure 2.17
Seed pod after
opening

or more. Those seeds which find themselves in a congenial environment will germinate in the spring and the cycle commences once more.

Identifying the species

Faced with the task of identifying an unknown plant people usually ask someone else, look through a book in the hope of recognising it from a picture or, if they are really serious about it, resort to the use of a key. Botanical keys ask you, as it were, to make a series of choices based on observations. These choices result in a process of elimination and lead you to a name for your plant. Provided your observations have been correct, this name should be the right one. The effectiveness of the key also depends to a considerable extent on the ability and experience of the person who composed it.

Already in the literature there is a number of keys to the species of *Wisteria*. For the commonly encountered species these work quite well. But for some of the rarely seen variants, they might

sometimes lead to a wrong conclusion. Hence I have constructed one of my own, no doubt not without its imperfections either, but I trust it is an improvement on earlier efforts.

This has been done following extensive observations over a long period, as a result of which I have found very few characteristics which can be reliably used to discriminate between species. For instance, it is often said that *W. sinensis,* the Chinese Wisteria, has fewer leaflets per leaf than *W. floribunda,* the Japanese Wisteria. This is generally true but, as there is considerable overlap, you could easily make a mistake if you were relying on this character to separate them.

Likewise it has frequently been written that in *W. sinensis* all the flowers in the raceme open simultaneously, whereas in *W. floribunda* they open in succession from the base. It has been my experience that the flowers open successively in all wisterias. It is just that in wisterias with few-flowered racemes a greater proportion of the flowers are open at once.

A Key to the Species

1. Twining anticlockwise.
   2. Standard, ovary and pods glabrous. Racemes terminal on well-developed leafy shoots in late spring.
      3. Leaflets 11–15. Racemes 4–8 cm with 25–65 flowers. Thick glandular hairs absent or only sparsely distributed on the rachis, pedicel and calyx.

      W. *frutescens* (L.) Poir.
      AMERICAN WISTERIA

      3.* Leaflets 7–11. Racemes up to 30 cm with up to 125 flowers. Thick glandular hairs frequent on the rachis, pedicel and calyx.

      W. *macrostachya* (Torr. & A. Gray) Nutt.
      KENTUCKY WISTERIA

   2.* Standard, ovary and pods pubescent. Racemes terminal on very short leafy shoots in spring.
      4. Pubescence confined to upper third of inner face of standard. Leaflets becoming almost glabrous. Racemes 12–35 cm with 25–95 flowers. Inflorescence buds in winter 4–5 mm × 2–3 mm.

      W. *sinensis* (Sims) Sweet
      CHINESE WISTERIA, ZI TENG

      4.* Pubescence extending to base of inner face of standard. Leaflets densely pubescent, remaining so at least below. Racemes 12–18 cm with up to 35 flowers. Inflorescence buds in winter 12–17 mm × 5–7 mm.

      W. *brachybotrys* Sieb. & Zucc.
      SILKY WISTERIA, YAMA FUJI
      (other than cv. 'Murasaki Kapitan)

1.* Twining clockwise.
   5. Standard, ovary and pods pubescent.
      6. Pubescence confined to upper third or less of inner face of standard. Racemes up to 50 cm or more with up to 170 flowers. Inflorescence buds in winter 5–7 mm × 2–2.5 mm.

      W. *floribunda* (Willd.) DC
      JAPANESE WISTERIA, FUJI, NODA FUJI

      6.* Pubescence extending to base of inner face of standard. Racemes 14–20 cm with 35–47 flowers. Inflorescence buds in winter 6–8 mm × 5–7 mm.

      W. *brachybotrys* Sieb. & Zucc. cv. 'Murasaki Kapitan'

   5.* Standard, ovary and pods glabrous. Racemes axillary on leafless peduncles or grouped as terminal panicles. Flowering in summer.

   Milletia *japonica* (Sieb. & Zucc.) A. Gray
   NATSU FUJI, SUMMER WISTERIA

To use this key start at the top and, on the basis of one or more of the characteristics mentioned, choose between 1 and 1* for the specimen concerned. Then choose between 2 and 2* or 5 and 5*, according to the choice made in the first place and so on. When a conclusion has been reached it can be confirmed by reading the detailed description of that species in the appropriate chapter and by looking at the illustrations.

Again it is said that W. *sinensis* blooms before the leaves expand whereas W. *floribunda* does so as the leaves become fully expanded. In reality leaf expansion and flowering begin simultaneously in both species. However as flowering goes on for longer in W. *floribunda,* there is time for the leaves to expand before all the flowers in the racemes have opened. Also, in both species the leaves expand more rapidly on non-flowering branches. I could go on.

There can be no confusion, however, with the direction of twining, provided it is observed correctly, nor with the size of the inflorescence buds in winter (figures 2.9–2.12) and the absence,

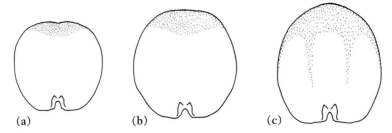

Figure 2.18 Distribution of hairs on the standard: (a) *Wisteria floribunda;*
(b) *Wisteria sinensis;* (c) *Wisteria brachybotrys*

presence, density, distribution and other characteristics of the minute hairs borne by many wisterias. In those species and cultivars which I have examined, the pubescence of the leaves, standard petal and ovary have proved useful distinguishing features.

As an example of this the distribution of hairs on the inner surface of the standard petal of *W. sinensis, W. floribunda* and *W. brachybotrys* is illustrated in figure 2.18. This characteristic can be observed with a hand lens in good light, as can the pubescence of the leaves.

Even so, at the present state of knowledge, it would be difficult to compose a foolproof key to all the species at present placed in the genus. Nevertheless it is hoped that the key below will prove useful to those wishing to distinguish the species encountered in cultivation. In this regard it is necessary to mention here that the author considers the name *W. brachybotrys* to be the correct one for the plant at present generally known in the West as *W. venusta*. This is discussed in chapter 5.

PLANT DESCRIPTIONS

In later chapters in order to describe the species and cultivars and to make comparisons, wherever possible the following information is given: time of blooming; number of leaflets per leaf; colour of the expanding leaves; characteristics of the pubescence of the leaves; time of leaf fall; and autumn colour. Also described are the abundance and size of the pods; the number of seeds per pod; and the colour and marking of the seeds. All measurements given are the result of observations made on at least ten specimens. The size, colour and pubescence of the inflorescence buds in winter has also been recorded. Particularly useful of course are the characteristics of the inflorescence. In order to make comparisons more meaningful, the length of the raceme has been taken to be the length of the rachis from the attachment of the first flower. By excluding the leafy peduncle in this way an additional source of variation is left out of consideration. The colour and other characteristics of the rachis, pedicel, calyx, standard, wings, keel, stamens and ovary have been recorded. Owing to the uneven colour of the flower parts and its tendency to vary according to conditions, no attempt has been made to define colour using any colour chart. It is hoped that general statements will suffice. Also, though every effort has been made with the photographs, it should be recognised that exact reproduction of colours with a predominance of blue is sometimes difficult to achieve.

CHAPTER 3

American Wisterias

As mentioned in chapter 1, the first wisteria to become known in Europe, and the one to which the generic name *Wisteria* was first applied, is *W. frutescens*, native to eastern North America. Later a second North American species was given the name *W. macrostachya*. It may yet be shown that these species merge into one another in nature but, since the forms in cultivation show horticulturally significant differences, they are dealt with separately here.

Wisteria frutescens (L.) Poir.   Figures 1.3, 3.2, 3.4

AMERICAN WISTERIA

According to *Hortus Third* (Bailey et al. 1976), *W. frutescens* is native to the south-eastern United States from Virginia to Florida. Alice Coats (1963) says that it was introduced to Britain in 1724 by Mark Catesby, the naturalist and artist who collected plants in Virginia from 1712 to 1719 and in Carolina, Florida and the Bahamas from 1722 to 1726. It was grown under the name of Carolina Kidney Bean, a name it received, according to Nuttall (1818), on account of its producing spotted seeds as large as the smaller kinds of kidney bean. Coats reports that the nurseryman Conrad Loddiges had a fine specimen trained on his house in Hackney, which flowered profusely in some years. Although it proved hardy, apparently it did not become widely grown. However, it must have attracted some notice, as it found its way to Australia and was listed in the 1843 catalogue of J. & W.

Figure 3.1   *Wisteria macrostachya*

Figure 3.2 *Wisteria frutescens*

Macarthur, Camden Park, NSW, the first nursery-man's catalogue known to have been printed in that country. It was listed again in their 1845 and 1850 catalogues and in the 1857 catalogue of John J. Rule in Victoria.

DESCRIPTION

There are several descriptions of this species in the literature, to which I add my own below, based on plants I have grown.

Slender vigorous climber, twining anticlock-wise. Leaves with 11–15 leaflets, glabrous on the upper surface except on the margins, hairs sparse below except on the veins. Flowers blue-violet, faintly scented, in racemes of 30–65, terminal on the current year's growth in late spring; floral bracts purple, deciduous; rachis green, pubescent, 4–7 cm long; pedicels pale green, pubescent, 6–8 mm long; calyx mauve, pubescent; occasional glandular hairs on various parts of the inflorescence; standard glabrous, 1.7–1.9 cm broad, with two membranous auricles at the base and a yellow blotch; wings each with a slender, pointed auricle above, as long as the claw, occasionally with a shorter and very fine auricle below as well; each element of the keel with a slender, pointed auricle shorter than the claw (figure 3.3); ovary, and subsequently the legume, glabrous. Autumn colour poor.

Rehder (1927, 1949) describes the wings as having 'a slender and a short auricle on either side' and Krüssman (1962) gives an unlabelled illustration showing a long slender auricle above the claw and a short one below. *The New RHS Dictionary of Gardening* (Huxley, Griffiths & Levy 1992) says 'wings with a short slender auricle on both sides' but what this means is not clear.

No doubt individuals and individual flowers occur with one or two auricles on each wing, as I have observed in the plant described above and in the closely related *W. macrostachya*. In addition to this the North American species differ from the Asian ones in having glabrous standards with thin and broadly triangular auricles, each wing with at least one narrow auricle as long as the claw, and glabrous ovaries. Also the wing petals tend to remain joined at their tips throughout flowering and do not separate readily as is often the case with the Asian species.

As might be expected there is considerable variation within *W. frutescens*. For instance there is a good form (figure 3.4) with darker flowers growing near the entrance to the conservatory at Longwood, Pennsylvania, and several cultivars have been named. These are discussed below.

Figure 3.3 *Wisteria frutescens*, flower structure

Figure 3.4 *Wisteria frutescens*, dark form at Longwood Gardens, Pennsylvania

CULTIVARS

'Alba'

See 'Nivea'.

'Albo-lilacina'

See *W. macrostachya*.

'Amethyst Falls'

A selected form found in Oconee County, South Carolina. There is a plant in the Arboretum of the North Carolina State University at Raleigh.

'Backhousiana'

According to Nicholson (1900) this had violet flowers in long compact racemes. It seems to have been lost and at any rate may have been a form of *W. macrostachya*. Presumably this was the plant listed in Australia as *Glycine backhousiana* in the 1857 Camden Park catalogue.

'Magnifica'

This was described by Nicholson (1900) as having clear blue flowers. *The New RHS Dictionary of Gardening* (Huxley, Griffiths & Levy 1992) says they are lilac with a large sulphur-yellow blotch on the standard. Nédélec (1992), on the other hand, describes it as having downy, clear blue flowers in racemes 15–20 cm long.

It appears that the name 'Magnifica' was applied last century to a long-racemed form or forms which would now be referred to *W. macrostachya*, which has longer racemes and also appears downier as a result of developing a larger proportion of thick glandular hairs on the pubescent regions of the inflorescence than does *W. frutescens,* at least in the forms seen in cultivation. Added to this, *Hortus Third* (Bailey et al. 1976) records *W. magnifica* as a name of no botanical standing referable to *W. macrostachya,* and Rehder (1949) lists *Glycine frutescens* var. *magnifica*

Hérincq and *W. frutescens magnifica* André, names published in the mid-nineteenth century in France, among the synonyms of that species. It is still listed as a cultivar of *W. frutescens* by French nurseries but does not seem any longer to be known elsewhere. At any rate, as indicated earlier, *W. frutescens* and *W. macrostachya* are very close to one another and it may eventually be decided that the names merely refer to extremes of a range of variation. Nevertheless, for horticultural purposes the maintenance of some differentiation is desirable.

'Nivea'   Figure 3.5

This was originally described in 1854 as *W. frutescens nivea* by Lescuyer and in 1903 as *W. frutescens* f. *nivea* (Lescuy.) Zabel (Rehder 1949). It is, however, deserving only of cultivar status. At times it has been known as 'Alba'.

It differs from the blue-violet form of the species described above in having a few hairs on the upper surfaces of the young leaflets, a greater proportion of glandular hairs on the pubescent parts of the inflorescence, pale green floral bracts and calyx, and flowers pure white except for a yellow blotch on the standard. The faintly scented

Figure 3.5   *Wisteria frutescens* 'Nivea'

flowers are borne in racemes of 25–55, the length of the rachis ranging from 3.9 to 9.5 cm.

'Purpurea'

According to Nicholson (1900), this had flowers of purple-violet. Along with 'Backhousiana' it seems to have disappeared.

'Rosea'

See *W. macrostachya* 'Albo-lilacina'.

'Swartley Purple'

Another selected form. There is a plant in the Arboretum of the North Carolina State University at Raleigh.

With its comparatively modest racemes and flowering as it does when the foliage is well developed, it is not surprising that *W. frutescens* has been passed over by many gardeners in favour of the more spectacular Asiatic species. All the same, flowering when these and their cultivars are finishing, it can be used to extend the season and, while vigorous, it is less invasive than the Asian species. In both its violet and white forms it has a charm of its own, and may well appeal to discerning gardeners on this account. Also, with the renewed enthusiasm for the growing of native plants, it is certainly deserving of wider cultivation in North America.

W. macrostachya (Torr. & A. Gray) Nutt.   Figures 3.1, 3.6

KENTUCKY WISTERIA

This plant was first described as a variety, *macrostachya*, of *W. frutescens* by Torrey and Gray (1838) on the basis of the name *W. macrostachya* used by Nuttall in an apparently unpublished manuscript. The epithet *macrostachya* means 'long spikes', in allusion to this wisteria having longer racemes than *W. frutescens*. One usually sees this plant listed as *W. macrostachya* (Torr. & A. Gray) Nutt. but it is hard to see why the authority for this name should be given in this form, since I have found no evidence that Nuttall was responsible for raising the varietal name published by Torrey and Gray to specific status. Rehder (1949) indicated that this was done by Robinson and Fernald (1908). However, in this reference it is given merely as *W. macrostachya* Nutt.

Stegermark (1963) lists it as *W. frutescens* (L.) Poir. var. *macrostachya* (Nutt.) Torr. & Gray, but goes on to say that 'Much of the Missouri material of *W. macrostachya* has the racemes of flowers only 7–12 cm long.' In other words short racemes are to be found frequently in *W. macrostachya* as well as in *W. frutescens*.

Another variation one encounters is that the specific epithet is spelled *macrostachys*. However this was not the spelling used by Torrey and Gray in the original publication of the name. None of this may be worth worrying about if people choose to follow authors such as Voss (1985), who includes it in *W. frutescens* without even assigning it varietal status.

If, as stated by Stegermark (1963), the length of the raceme cannot be reliably used to distinguish the American species, the abundance of club-shaped glands on the calyx and pedicels in *W. macrostachya*, in contrast with their lack or scarcity in *W. frutescens,* is the only character left for separation in the key given by Fernald (1950), whereas in Gleason and Cronquist (1963) the two are separated by 'upper lip of the calyx less than half as long as the tube' in *W. frutescens* as contrasted with 'upper lip of the calyx nearly or fully as long as the tube' in *W. macrostachya*.

These observations concerning the calyx certainly do not apply to material I have seen, the

Figure 3.6   *Wisteria macrostachya*

upper lip of the calyx being much the same size in both species. Also since club-shaped glandular hairs occur in both species, it is hard to see how these can be relied upon as a character to distinguish them. No doubt the problem will be resolved, if it has not been already, by the examination of a range of material from the whole of the habitat. Meanwhile, I have decided to follow *Hortus Third* (Bailey et al. 1976) and *The New RHS Dictionary of Gardening* (Huxley, Griffiths & Levy 1992) and keep *W. macrostachya* separate and use the authority citation (Torrey & A. Gray) Nutt. until all this is sorted out.

W. macrostachya occurs in swamps from Louisiana north to Illinois and blooms later in the season than *W. frutescens,* and is useful on that account. Introductions from the northern part of its range may well tolerate lower temperatures.

As mentioned earlier, it seems to have come to notice as a garden plant in France in the middle of last century, being described as a long-racemed form, *magnifica*, of *W. frutescens*. It seems probable that this introduction is the cultivar 'Magnifica' discussed previously under *W. frutescens* and still offered by French nurseries (Nédélec 1992).

DESCRIPTION

The description given below is of a plant obtained in 1990 from the Louisiana Nursery.

Slender vigorous climber, twining anticlockwise. Leaves with 7–11 leaflets, usually 9, rapidly becoming glabrous on the upper surface except at the margins, hairs scattered below, denser on veins. Flowers pale violet, faintly scented, in racemes of 70–80, terminal on current year's growth in late spring; floral bracts pale green, edged and tipped mauve, deciduous; rachis green, 15–20 cm long, pubescent, a few of the hairs glandular; pedicels pale green, tinged mauve in strong light, 8–9 mm long, pubescent with some hairs glandular; calyx reddish purple, darker than the petals, pubescent with some hairs glandular; standard 1.8–2.2 cm broad, yellow blotched, with two flat triangular auricles at the base, glabrous; wings darker than standard and keel, each with two slender pointed auricles, the upper as long as the claw, the lower a little shorter or with only one long upper auricle; keel elements each with a short thick auricle; ovary, and subsequently legume, glabrous (figure 3.7). Autumn colour yellowish green.

It must be noted that this description applies only to a cultivated plant and that in nature considerable variation in colour and other characters occurs. Nevertheless the most obvious differences from *W. frutescens* appear to be fewer leaflets per leaf, more flowers per raceme, and a greater proportion of glandular hairs on the pubescent parts of the inflorescence. Frequently also the first one or two flowers of the raceme are produced in the axils of leaves, a phenomenon not seen in *W. frutescens*. It is interesting that the raceme length is the same as that given by Nédélec (1992) for *W. frutescens* 'Magnifica'. Apart from this plant, cultivars of *W. macrostachya* appear to have become available again only recently as the result of the introduction of selected forms.

Figure 3.7 *Wisteria macrostachya*, flower structure. Note wing petal with two auricles

CULTIVARS

'Abbeville Blue' — Figure 3.8

In its general characteristics this resembles the species described above but has pale blue-violet flowers in racemes of up to 90; rachis up to 25 cm long; floral bracts mauve; wing petals consistently 2-auricled. It is a vigorous healthy grower but is easy to train and keep within bounds. This fine cultivar was found near the mouth of the Vermillion River near the Gulf of Mexico and named and introduced by the Louisiana Nursery.

'Albo-lilacina'

According to Rehder (1949), this was originally described as *W. frutescens* c. *albo-lilacina* by Dippel in 1893, who gave *W. frutescens rosea* as a synonym. It was raised to the status of a botanical form of *W. macrostachya* by Rehder (1926a), who said that it had pale lilac flowers. It seems to have disappeared.

'Bayou Two O'Clock'

As for the species described above but with blue-violet flowers in racemes up to 25 cm long. This excellent blue cultivar was selected by Sylvan D'Avy on the Two O'Clock Bayou in southern Louisiana. According to the Louisiana Nursery, who named and introduced it, it can grow in shallow water as well as regular garden soil.

'Clara Mack'

As for the species described above but with white flowers in slightly shorter and fuller racemes. It also has slightly broader leaflets than the other cultivars described here. This rare white form of the Kentucky Wisteria blooms prolifically.

'Pondside Blue' — Figure 3.9

As for the species described above but with 115–125 flowers of light blue-violet in racemes 23–30 cm long; floral bracts pale green, tinged mauve, deciduous; rachis green, 23–30 cm, pubescent, with some glandular hairs; calyx greenish white, tinged mauve towards the lobes; wings each with a single slender pointed auricle as long as the claw; keel elements each with a shorter pointed auricle.

This cultivar differs from the form of the species described previously in its bluer flowers, the pubescent parts of the raceme being more conspicuously glandular-hairy, the racemes being longer and with more flowers, and in the wings each having only one auricle. As mentioned earlier it seems there is variation in this characteristic in both *W. frutescens* and *W. macrostachya*, some individuals having one, others two. Also, up to the first four flowers in the raceme may be borne in the axils of leaves, and occasionally in the axil of the first leaf of the raceme there is a two-flowered sub-raceme.

According to the Louisiana Nursery, who selected and named it, it will grow well even in wet soil or near water.

From the descriptions given and the accompanying illustrations, it should be clear that the *W. macrostachya* and its cultivars have considerable potential as garden ornaments, particularly for their ease of control, tolerance of wet soils, late flowering and long racemes. As regards the number of flowers per raceme, they rival many of the forms of *W. floribunda*. So it is to be hoped we shall see a lot more of *W. macrostachya* and its cultivars. And, as well as admiring the appearance of the blooms, it seems you can bring them into the kitchen, as, according to Stegermark (1963), the fresh flowers may be eaten as a salad or cooked in batter as fritters. Presumably those of *W. frutescens* can be treated similarly.

Figure 3.9 *above*
Wisteria macrostachya
'Pondside Blue'

Figure 3.8 *left*
Wisteria macrostachya
'Abbeville Blue'

CHAPTER 4

Chinese Wisterias

Wisteria sinensis (Sims) Sweet

CHINESE WISTERIA, ZI TENG

CULTIVATION OUTSIDE CHINA

Whether trained on a wall or pergola, allowed to ramble through trees or over fences, pruned to form a shrub or standard, or even grown in a pot, the Chinese Wisteria must be one of the most appealing plants of all time. For drawing attention to the first known mention of this plant by a European, we are indebted to Emil Bretschneider, who was stationed at Beijing as physician to the Russian legation from 1866 to 1883. Bretschneider became greatly interested in the Chinese flora and after his return published his painstaking *History of European Botanical Discoveries in China* (1898). In this he records that in a letter from Domenicus Parennin, a French Jesuit missionary who went to China in 1698 and died in Beijing in 1741, Parennin mentions 'the climbing plant *teng lo* with beautiful violet flowers hanging down in large bunches. This is *Wistaria chinensis*'.

In and around Beijing the plant is still occasionally referred to as Teng Lo, which seems to be a local name. Both 'teng' and 'lo (luo)' refer to climbing plants, so Teng Lo is perhaps best translated as 'climbing vine'. Its botanical name in Chinese is Zi Teng, meaning 'violet vine', and is the name generally used. Rehder and Wilson (1916) say the plant is known colloquially in western Hubei as Chiao Teng (or Qiao Teng, in Pinyin), perhaps merely meaning 'beautiful vine', although one would have to see the original character

Figure 4.1 *Wisteria sinensis*, typical form

romanised as 'chiao' and hear it pronounced to be certain. It may well be that the plant has or has had other names elsewhere in China.

The Chinese Wisteria was not brought to Europe until 1816, and was first described by John Sims (1819) as *Glycine sinensis*, on account of its close similarity to *G. frutescens* of Linnaeus, although he was aware that it was not a 'proper *Glycine*' and that Nuttall had established the separate genus *Wisteria* for the American species in 1818. Nevertheless Sims decided to retain the name *Glycine* as, until fruits could be examined, he felt 'it must be uncertain where it ought to be arranged'. Eventually, just as Poiret had transferred *G. frutescens* to Nuttall's genus *Wisteria* 1823, so in 1827 Robert Sweet transferred *G. sinensis* (Rehder 1949). Thus the currently accepted citation is *W. sinensis* (Sims) Sweet, even though botanists from time to time have given it other names, now regarded as synonyms.

The specimen upon which Sims based his description was brought to him by Alexander Macleay from the garden of Charles Hampden Turner of Rooksnest, Surrey, to whom it had been brought from Guangzhou (Canton) in May 1816 by Captain Welbank, then commanding the East Indiaman 'Cufnells'. Apparently the plant had had a dreadful time after its arrival, as it was kept in the peach house at 30°C, where it was nearly killed by red spider (two-spotted mite). Upon reduction of the heat it recovered somewhat and, after being kept for the winter in a greenhouse where the temperature dropped below freezing on occasions, it bloomed for the first time in the spring of 1819. Sims records that the gardener had propagated it by both layers and cuttings, and proposed to test its hardiness out of doors.

The early history of its cultivation in England has been documented by Joseph Sabine (1826), who states that, a few days after the arrival of Mr Turner's plant in 1816, another was brought by

Captain Richard Rawes to Thomas Carey Palmer of Bromley, with whom it too first blossomed in 1819. Also, according to Sabine, the original plants were obtained from a vine in the garden of Consequa, a Guangzhou merchant.

Sabine records that the first propagations from Mr Turner's plant were given to the Horticultural Society and to Messrs Loddiges at Hackney, and that those from Mr Palmer's were presented to Lady Long and to Mr Lee of Hammersmith. He goes on to say that 'each of these, together with the original plants, have for the last three or four years been objects of admiration to all who have seen them'.

Sabine also noted that the plants frequently put out a small second crop of flowers on the young shoots of the year, immediately after the spring blossoming is past, but that these are not so fine as the first crop of flowers, though they are darker in colour. This phenomenon seems to be widespread among wisterias, the early summer flowers usually differing a little in colour from those of the main spring flowering.

In addition to the introductions mentioned above, it is said (Bretschneider 1898; Wilson 1916; and others) that a plant of *W. sinensis* was sent from the same source to the Horticultural Society's garden at Chiswick in 1818 by John Reeves, who it seems likely had been instrumental in obtaining the earlier plants. Whether he really sent a plant in 1818 or whether the Horticultural Society's plant was, as mentioned above, the one propagated from Mr Turner's plant remains uncertain. However it is known for certain that about that time Reeves sent a watercolour made of it in China (figure 4.2). This depicts a summer raceme borne terminally on a shoot of the current year.

Figure 4.2
Wisteria sinensis, from the *Reeves Collection of Chinese Drawings*, volume 2, number 64 (Lindley Library, Royal Horticultural Society)

Whatever its origin the Horticultural Society's plant at Chiswick attracted a deal of attention. Dr John Lindley (1840), for instance, was moved to observe that 'a magnificent specimen of this plant, 180 feet [about 55 m] long, and covering about 1800 square feet [167 m²] of wall, has been for some time an object of great interest in the garden of the Horticultural Society, where hundreds of persons have visited it and admired its piles of lilac-coloured fragrant flowers. The following little calculation will serve to shew how wonderful is the evidence afforded by this single specimen of the creative power of Nature.

'The number of branches was about 9000 and of flowers 675,000. Each flower consisting of 5 petals, the number of these parts was 3,375,000. Each flower contained 10 stamens, or the whole mass of flowers 6,750,000. Each ovary contained about 7 ovules, so that preparation was made for the production of 4,050,000 seeds, for the purpose of fertilising which the anthers, if perfect, would have contained 27,000,000,000 pollen grains. Had all the petals been placed end to end they would have extended to the distance of more than *thirty-four miles* [about 55 km].'

While his mathematics do not bear too close an examination, it is clear that the plant had a profound effect on him and no doubt on others, for, although it had remained unknown outside China for so long, it soon found its way to the gardens of most of the rest of the temperate world.

Sabine (1826) says that a plant growing in the 'late garden' of Alexander Macleay at Tilbuster Lodge in Surrey survived the winter unprotected and bloomed, so proving it to be hardy there. It evidently had impressed Macleay too, as, after his arrival in Sydney as Colonial Secretary in 1825, it was the first plant listed by him as received for the extensive garden he established on the 54 acres of land granted to him in 1826 at Elizabeth Bay (Stackhouse 1981). Thus it seems likely he

was the first to introduce it to Australia, where it was listed in the catalogues of nurserymen by mid-century. Along with *W. frutescens*, it appeared in the Camden Park catalogue of 1843, in 1845 in the catalogue of James Dixon of Hobart, the first catalogue known from Tasmania, and in the 1855 catalogue of J. & J. Rule, the first catalogue known from Victoria.

It has been suggested that there is no evidence that it was taken to Japan, in spite of the proximity of this country to China, until early this century, although misconceptions can arise about this owing to earlier authors assuming the Japanese Wisteria to belong to the same species, calling it *Glycine sinensis*, *W. chinensis* or *W. sinensis*. Wilson (1916) says that 'in Japan, where it was unknown, even as a cultivated plant until recently, it has been introduced, and is now grown and sold by the Yokohama Nursery Company'. Even so, it is still rarely encountered. No doubt the popularity of the indigenous wisterias accounts for this.

The statements made in the above paragraph aside, among the ancient wisterias in Japan which have been accorded the status of National Treasure, is the Miyazaki-jingu-no-o-shira-fuji (meaning 'the big white wisteria of the Miyazaki Shrine'). According to Kawarada (1985) this is the largest and oldest Chinese Wisteria in Japan, reputedly planted 600 years ago. If this really is a Chinese Wisteria then this species has, as one might expect, been in Japan for a long time and as a white variant at that.

While it might seem extraordinary that it took so long for this spectacular plant to reach Europe, it must be remembered that, unless, like the peach and apricot, it had made its way across the trade route of the Silk Road, the discovery of most Chinese plants by Europeans had to await their arrival in China by sea. Even then, although the Portuguese had settled in Macau in the sixteenth century, it was not until the eighteenth century that trade with foreign powers became established in Guangzhou, to which from 1757 all trade was restricted.

In Guangzhou, foreigners were allowed to reside only on a narrow strip of riverbank and only from November to May each year, without their wives or any foreign women, and to trade with a limited number of licensed traders. Under these circumstances, and since Guangzhou is in the tropics, it is surprising that as many plants from the temperate parts of China reached Europe as did in the eighteenth century and the early part of the nineteenth. It seems, however, that many plants such as tree peonies, camellias and chrysanthemums were brought from nurseries further north for sale in Guangzhou, as they still are. Thus it was that many such plants were grown in glasshouses in Europe before they were found to be hardy out of doors. But the richness of China's wild and cultivated flora didn't begin to be fully appreciated until the opening up of the country in the middle of the nineteenth century.

It was at the beginning of this period that the white form of *W. sinensis* (figures 4.28–4.29) was met with by Robert Fortune, who had been sent to China as a collector for the Horticultural Society. He first encountered it in Ningbo in 1844 growing on a flat trellis with the normal form. 'Entwined with one of these trees,' he wrote (1847), 'I found another variety having very long racemes of pure white flowers, which contrasted well with the light blue of the other. I obtained permission from the old Chinese gentleman to whom it belonged (my old friend Dr Chang) to make some layers of this fine plant, and I am happy to say that one of these is now alive in the garden at Chiswick.' He was also able to obtain a white form from a nursery garden in Suzhou, but whether it was the same as the one from Ningbo and what happened to it is uncertain.

After this there appear to have been very few introductions of wisterias from China. Whereas, after establishment of trade with the West, Japanese nurserymen quickly realised there was a market for their plants abroad and produced catalogues in English, the Chinese did not. Ernest Wilson (1916) pointed out that almost all plants of *W. sinensis* in cultivation outside China had descended from the original introductions and that there was no evidence to prove that any others had since been brought to Europe. He records that the only plant of independent origin of which he knew was one on a house on the edge of the Arnold Arboretum in Boston, raised from seeds received from Shanghai in 1887.

Much the same situation still exists. Almost all the violet Chinese Wisterias in cultivation outside China appear to belong to the one clone. This is not surprising as it rarely sets seed in most climates, though here and there minor variations (figure 4.3) have turned up and occasionally have been given cultivar names. Recently I have raised plants from seeds collected in Zhejiang and distributed by the Shanghai Botanical Garden. Some of these have bloomed and in general they resemble the original introduction, varying in depth of colour and, in some cases, having flowers of a more pinkish violet.

It is clear that most people outside China have an incomplete picture of the range of variation in *W. sinensis*. Hence in the section of this chapter which follows I have attempted to make some amends.

DISTRIBUTION AND VARIATION IN CHINA

The only person so far to have recorded any mention of the range of variation of *W. sinensis* in the wild appears, again, to be Wilson (1913), who wrote of the plants growing wild near Yichang, Hubei, that the flowers were borne in great

Figure 4.3 *Wisteria sinensis,* pale form at Greys Court, Oxfordshire

Figure 4.4
Wisteria sinensis, pale
form, Zhejiang

Figure 4.5
Wisteria sinensis, typical
form, Zhejiang

Figure 4.6
Wisteria sinensis, dark
form, Beijing

abundance and varied very much in shade of colour, the white form being, however, rather rare.

I was able to make a similar observation on a trip of almost 300 km from Hangzhou, Zhejiang, to Huangshan, Anhui, in April 1994, when many plants were seen in bloom on the hillsides. There was considerable variation in the length of raceme and in colour of the flowers, which ranged from palest blue-violet, violet and reddish violet to much deeper shades of the same colours. No white forms, however, were seen. Colour variations seen both in the wild and in cultivation in China are illustrated in figures 4.4–4.7 and 4.21.

Likewise in cultivation in Shanghai, Suzhou, Hangzhou, Huangshan and Beijing, no two plants appeared to be the same. Except for the rarely seen white forms, all presumably had been raised from seed or dug from the wild.

Sabine (1826) had early pointed out that it was probably a native of some parts of the Chinese empire distant from Guangzhou. But as to where *W. sinensis* occurs naturally it is hard to be

Figure 4.7 *Wisteria sinensis*, reddish
violet form, Shi Zi Lin, Suzhou

at all clear. For a start many of the subsequent records and collections are of cultivated plants from various parts of the country. Then, since much of the China has been subjected to human interference for thousands of years, and since this wisteria seems usually to occur spontaneously only at low altitudes, it is impossible to know whether the locations where it is growing are part of its original habitat or areas where it has become naturalised.

As far as I know the first European record of *W. sinensis* growing apparently naturally is that of Robert Fortune (1847), who met it for the first time on the island of Zhoushan. As he later (1852) writes: 'At this place, and all over the provinces of Chekiang and Kiang-nan, the Glycine seemed to be at home. It grew wild on every hillside, scrambling about in hedges by the footpaths, and hanging over and dipping its leaves and flowers into the canals and mountain streams.'

Fortune (1852) was shown a beautiful specimen in a ruined garden on an island near Xiamen, but noted that it did not occur in a wild state there and had evidently been brought from more northern latitudes. He commented that 'it is not indigenous to the south of China, and is rarely seen in perfection there. Indeed the simple fact of its being perfectly hardy in England shows at once that it had a more northern origin.'

Wilson (1916) noted *W. sinensis* to be not uncommon at low altitudes in western Hubei and eastern Sichuan but that it was rare in western Sichuan, even in gardens, and that there was no record of it growing wild in the regions north of Shanghai. He collected it from Yichang, western Hubei, at 30–500 m, in April 1907, noting it to be fairly common on cliffs and trees, often scaling high trees, though the semi-bush form was more common (Wilson 1913; Rehder & Wilson 1916).

Rehder and Wilson also list a specimen collected by Faber in Jiangsu, and Rehder (1926b) subsequently lists collections from Shandong, Shaanxi and Henan. He also says it occurs in Hubei, Jiangsu, Zhejiang, Guangdong and Sichuan, but in many instances the records are of cultivated plants.

As recently as 1983, Lancaster (1989) found

W. sinensis to be abundant on the slopes of Wudang Shan in north-west Hubei. And, as already mentioned, in April 1994 I was able to see it growing on uncultivated hillsides, roadsides and streambanks in those parts of Zhejiang and Anhui through which I passed, flowering at the same time as *Rosa laevigata, Rhododendron simsii, R. ovatum* and the occasional yellow *R. molle*. It was easily detected, even at a distance, on account of its conspicuous floral display and, in the case of non-flowering plants, by the coppery young foliage. As with Lancaster's observations in Hubei, no large plants were seen, perhaps as a result of the regular lopping of the scrub. The only large plants which I saw climbing up and over trees were in the wooded areas around temples and these, of course, may have been planted originally.

Whether *W. sinensis* occurs naturally anywhere in the far south is not known, but perhaps it may occasionally be found there at higher altitudes. Likewise in northern China in 1923 F. N. Meyer collected a wisteria in fruit near Qinhuangdao, Hebei, among high scrub, apparently genuinely wild. This specimen was included by Rehder and Wilson (1916) in their new species, *W. venusta*, and later transferred by Rehder (1926b) to *W. villosa*, the identity of which is discussed later in this chapter. Rehder stated that there were no specimens of *W. sinensis* from northern China in the herbarium at the Arnold Arboretum and that a specimen collected in Shandong was probably cultivated, as it was said to occur in villages. More recently Lancaster (1989) reported what he assumed to be *W. sinensis*, doubtfully native, from the Fragrant Hills near Beijing, growing in and over a variety of trees, where it was easy to see the anticlockwise direction of its twining stems. Whether it is genuinely native anywhere in northern China I do not know.

While a tour round almost the whole of China would be needed for an adequate assessment to be made of the spontaneous occurrence and range of variation of *W. sinensis*, it seems likely that its principal distribution is in central and eastern areas, perhaps extending south at higher altitudes and north at low altitudes in the east. I saw no trace of it in May 1994 in South Korea, where *W. floribunda* is widespread at low altitudes, occurring in habitats similar to those occupied by *W. sinensis* in eastern China.

CULTIVATION IN CHINA

It is clear from the foregoing that *W. sinensis* is widely cultivated in China. It was introduced to England from a cultivated plant, Fortune saw it cultivated in numerous places, and Wilson (1916) and Rehder and Wilson (1916) remarked that 'it is much cultivated in Shanghai, Soo-chou, Han-chou, and other centres of wealth and culture in eastern China'. I have seen it cultivated in Kunming and in almost every park and garden visited in Shanghai, Suzhou, Hangzhou, the Huangshan area in Anhui, and Beijing.

Presumably the plant has been admired and cultivated in China for a long time. Uehara (1961) says it is often mentioned in old Chinese poems, including one by the esteemed Pai Lo-tien (772–846), known in Japan by the name Hakurakuten. There is a photograph in the collection of the Arnold Arboretum taken by F. N. Meyer in September 1907 at Tai'an, Shandong, and labelled 'One of the largest wisterias in the world, growing in the courtyard of the Ta Miais ('Big Temple'). This specimen is several centuries old.' And in May 1994 I was taken to see another old vine at Zi Teng Peng Zeng ('Wisteria Pergola Village') on the south-west outskirts of Shanghai. It is said to have been planted 480 years ago in the Ming dynasty. It originally grew along a street of old shops and the scene must have been charming. Recently it has been declared an item of heritage significance, the old shops have been

Figure 4.8   Ancient wisteria at Zi Teng Peng Zeng

removed in case they burn down and destroy it, and it has been provided with a modern pergola in contemporary taste (figure 4.8).

While I have made no special search, the earliest illustration of a cultivated wisteria in China that I have come across is in a painting of one of the forty scenes at Yuan Ming Yuan painted by T'ang Tai and Shen Yuan in 1744 for the Emperor Ch'ienlung, now in the Bibliothèque Nationale in Paris. Scene number seven, *Merciful Clouds All Protecting,* shows, among other things, a wisteria in full bloom on a pergola in front of a pavilion (figure 4.9), along with tree peonies and flowering peaches, all of which can be seen in bloom at the same time in Beijing today. There may be earlier examples, such as the vines shown growing on trellis fences in seventeenth-century scrolls reproduced by Osvald Sirén (1949, plates 1 & 91), which might possibly be interpreted as stylised representations of wisteria.

Perhaps an extensive survey of Chinese literature and art would reveal more of its horticultural history. For instance Li (1959) gives a bibliography of over one hundred Chinese works about plants and gardens from before 1850, some dating back to the third century AD. He records mention of wisteria in 1406 in the *Famine Herbal* (a book describing plants which can be eaten

when nothing better is available), reproducing an illustration of a flowering branch (figure 4.10).

It seems unlikely that so conspicuous and charming a plant would not have attracted attention from early times. However it does not seem to have been favoured as a subject in literature and painting or as a decorative motif to the same extent that many other Chinese plants have, nor become invested to the same degree with symbolic associations. This is in marked contrast to the treatment of wisteria in Japan. On the other hand, with its sinuous branches, pendulous racemes and elegantly arranged leaves, it was recognised in the United States as a suitable subject for depiction in the Art Nouveau style by Louis Comfort Tiffany, whose stained glass windows and lamps are widely admired (figure 4.11).

Nowadays at least, there do not seem to be named cultivars of wisteria in China, unless of course the white ones have names. This too is in contrast to the situation in Japan where there are many cultivars of *W. floribunda* and *W. brachybotrys*. Perhaps vegetatively propagated

cultivars existed in the past but were lost during the turbulent years of this century, particularly during the Cultural Revolution when the cultivation of plants for ornament was not viewed with favour. Nevertheless, as those who have grown them will know, wisterias are very hard to kill and there are many plants in Chinese gardens which appear to be of considerable age, even if recently regrown from substantial stumps. As with younger plants, no two of these appear to be the same, and presumably they too were raised from seed or dug from the wild.

Wisterias are grown in Chinese gardens in a number of ways. Fortune (1852) felt that 'by far the most beautiful effect is produced when it attaches itself to the stems and branches of trees. This is not infrequent in nature, and is often copied by the Chinese and introduced to their gardens.' He also remarked that 'the Chinese are fond of growing the Glycine on trellis-work, and forming long covered walks in the garden, or arbours or porticos in front of their doors', and that in the azalea gardens in Shanghai there was 'a specimen of *Wistaria chinensis* in a dwarfed state

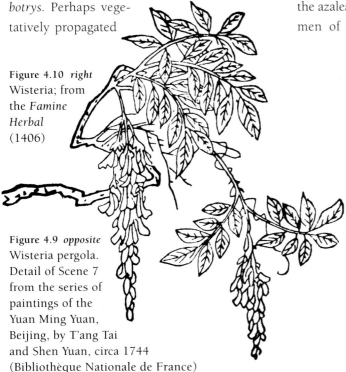

Figure 4.10 *right*
Wisteria; from the *Famine Herbal* (1406)

Figure 4.9 *opposite*
Wisteria pergola. Detail of Scene 7 from the series of paintings of the Yuan Ming Yuan, Beijing, by T'ang Tai and Shen Yuan, circa 1744 (Bibliothèque Nationale de France)

Figure 4.11 Wisteria lamps
by Louis Comfort Tiffany

Figure 4.12   Wisteria portico, Liwangfu, Beijing, 1922 (Osvald Sirén)

Figure 4.13   Wisteria portico, Gongwangfu, Beijing, 1994

Figure 4.14   Wisteria bridge, Liu Yuan, Suzhou, circa 1935 (Osvald Sirén)

growing in a pot. The tree was evidently aged, from the size of its stem. It was about six feet [1.8 m] high, the branches came out from the stem in a regular and symmetrical manner, and it had the appearance of a tree in miniature. Every one of the branches was now loaded with long racemes of pendulous lilac blossoms. These hung down from the horizontal branches, and gave the whole the appearance of a floral fountain.'

The photographs of Osvald Sirén (1949), from the twenties and thirties, show a wisteria growing up a tree, on a wooden pergola, over a wooden portico (figure 4.12), on a wooden bridge (figure 4.14) and over a rockery (figure 4.16).

Sir Osbert Sitwell (1935), writing in England after a visit to the Summer Palace in Beijing, says that 'the cultivation of wisteria, too, has attained in China a degree of excellence unknown here, and the blossom is treated in various and original ways. Sometimes an old vine is hung through

Figure 4.15   Wisteria bridge, Liu Yuan, Suzhou, 1994

a lattice, so that each drooping head is framed in a square; sometimes a stout tree has its serpentine branches supported by painted props of wood which look as though they were fashioned of coral, or, again, it is encouraged to writhe over a shallow pool so that it may be mirrored the better.'

Figure 4.16   Wisteria growing over piled rocks, Zhonghai, Beijing, 1922 (Osvald Sirén)

Figure 4.17   Wisteria growing over piled rocks, Liu Yuan, Suzhou, 1994

While I have not seen a plant supported by painted props, nor one hung through a lattice so that each drooping head is framed in a square, the other styles of cultivation are still to be seen. In and around Beijing wisterias are commonly planted to grow up trees (figure 4.18); there is a wisteria covered portico at Gongwangfu, Beijing (figure 4.13); the wisteria bridge shown in Osvald Sirén's photograph is still there in the Liu Yuan, Suzhou (figure 4.15); plants trained over rock piles are to be seen in Shanghai, Suzhou and Hangzhou (figure 4.17); others hang over the edges of ponds; and pergolas of bamboo, wood, iron and concrete occur widely.

As might be expected, it is the bamboo pergolas that most please Western eyes. Very often they are arched, as in the case of an elaborate one beside a canal in Suzhou (figure 4.19), a smaller version of which can be seen in Zhuo Zheng Yuan in the same city (figure 4.20). A concrete version of this style is to be seen supporting a white wisteria in the Yu Yuan, Shanghai. Other plants are trained as shrubs (figure 4.21), sometimes with a background of trellis work, and as penjing (figure 4.22), the Chinese method of producing miniaturised plants in containers, an art form dating back at least 2000 years (Hu 1988).

Figure 4.18   Wisteria growing over a juniper, Beijing Botanical Garden

Figure 4.19   Wisteria pergola beside a canal, Suzhou

Figure 4.20   Wisteria pergola, Zhuo Zheng Yuan, Suzhou

Figure 4.21 White wisteria, Huanglongsi, Hangzhou

Figure 4.22 *Wisteria sinensis* as penjing

POISONOUS PROPERTIES

According to Cornevin (1893), *W. sinensis* has been accused of causing migraines, nausea, vertigo and nervous disorders, yet extracts of the branches and leaves collected in summer and autumn, whether aqueous or alcoholic, had no effect on experimental animals. As result he presumed it to be toxic only at the beginning of the season before flowering. However Kingsbury (1964) and Oehme (1978) record that severe gastrointestinal symptoms followed ingestion of the pods and seeds. As reported by Everist (1981), the pods and seeds contain a resin and a glycoside, wisterin, and have caused poisoning in children in many countries, producing mild to severe gastroenteritis. In China the poisonous properties of the seeds is sometimes exploited by using an extract as an insecticide.

USE AS FOOD AND MEDICINE

In view of the foregoing it would be wise to be cautious in treating the plant as a comestible. On the other hand the fact that it is listed in the *Famine Herbal* of 1406 indicates that the flowers or some other part of the plant could be eaten with impunity. More recently Du Cane (1908) and Wyman (1949) mention the eating of the flowers by the Chinese, and Meng Rengong of the Beijing Botanical Garden tells me that the parboiled flowers are eaten fried and also that, after curing with sugar they are mixed with flour and made into teng lo cake, a famous delicacy. Apparently the young leaves may be eaten as well.

Armed with the above information a friend of mine has used individual flowers glazed with olive oil to enliven the appearance of green salads. Neither he nor his guests have come to any obvious harm. Nor, I assume, has anyone following Stegermark's (1963) similar suggestion concerning *W. macrostachya,* as reported in the preceding chapter.

Meng Rengong also reports that the seeds, stems and flowers of *W. sinensis* are also used in Chinese medicine. Obviously the seeds must be used with great care on account of their toxic properties.

DESCRIPTION

As mentioned earlier, the original description of the *W. sinensis* was based on a single cultivated specimen introduced from Guangzhou, and subsequent descriptions appear to be based on the same clone. Here I propose to broaden this by describing the species as seen recently in China.

As seen south of the Yangtze (Chiang Jiang)   Figs 4.4, 4.5, 4.7, 4.21

Vigorous deciduous climber, twining anticlockwise. Leaves up to 30 cm long with 9–13 leaflets; leaflets ovate-elliptic to oblong, to 10 cm long, usually copper- or bronze-green when young, pubescent, the hairs longer above, shorter and more dense below, becoming almost glabrous above but hairs remaining below, particularly on and near the veins. Inflorescence buds in winter 5.0–7.0 mm × 2.5–3.0 mm, pointed, the outer two bracts dark reddish brown, shortly hairy on the outer surfaces, almost completely covering the inner bracts at first. Flowers blue-violet, violet or reddish violet, pale to dark, rarely white, scented, appearing with the leaves in racemes of 25–95; floral bracts small, deciduous, pubescent, usually tinged violet; rachis green, pubescent, 12–35 cm long; pedicels 1.5–2.5 cm, pubescent, often suffused violet; calyx pubescent, usually violet, lower three lobes pointed; standard 1.8–2.5 cm broad, auricled, pubescent at the top on its inner surface, outer surface glabrous or with a few hairs around the claw, blotch variable in width, one-half to two-thirds the height of the standard, yellow or green edged with white, fading; wings each with a short pointed auricle, apex rounded; keel

elements each with a pointed auricle, apex with an obtuse point; stamens 10, glabrous, 9 joined, 1 free; ovary pubescent, developing into a woody velutinous legume with one or more flattened brown seeds heavily spotted, mottled and streaked black (figures 4.23–4.24).

Not having been in China in the autumn, I cannot comment on the colour of the leaves before falling. However among the cultivars the colour ranges from poor to a quite good yellow. Plants raised from seeds sent by the Shanghai Botanic Garden have leaves which turn a good clear yellow.

Forms occur in China which differ from one another almost as much as do the cultivars of *W. floribunda* in Japan. Hence the selection and introduction to cultivation elsewhere of long-racemed pale and dark forms seems desirable. There is, for instance, in the Yu Yuan, Shanghai, a beautiful reddish violet form with up to 95 flowers in the raceme, the standard having a narrow green blotch, edged with white (figure 4.25). It would also be worth searching for pink variants and for white ones of a purer colour and with stronger pedicels than those at present in cultivation.

As seen in cultivation in and around Beijing   Figures 4.18, 4.26, 4.33

In general appearance much as those seen south of the Yangtze; twining anticlockwise, leaves sometimes a little larger, rarely showing any bronze colouration when young. Racemes usually longer, 20–35 cm, hanging vertically in the manner of *W. floribunda,* the flowers violet to reddish violet, ranging from pale to quite strongly coloured, usually further apart, the effect heightened by the pedicels being longer, 2.0–3.2 cm; standard usually about 2.5 cm broad, the margins often remaining somewhat incurved, the blotch yellow and white or white, large, with its

Figure 4.23 *Wisteria sinensis,*
flower structure

Figure 4.25 Long-racemed form of *Wisteria sinensis* at Yu Yuan, Shanghai

Figure 4.24 Seeds of *Wisteria sinensis*

margin clearly delimited in colour from the rest of the standard (figures 4.6, 4.27). Seeds brown, heavily spotted, mottled and streaked black.

While the Beijing forms are recognisably different, at least from a horticultural point of view, from the southern ones, the differences do not seem to be much if any greater than those between the white forms seen in the south and in cultivation elsewhere, with their long racemes and weak pedicels, and the usual violet forms.

While in Beijing I was able to examine over thirty different plants in bloom in the Beijing Botanic Garden, the Temple of the Sleeping Buddha (Wofosi), the Temple of the Azure Clouds

Figure 4.26 *Wisteria sinensis*, Beijing type, showing the long racemes and pedicels and the widely spaced flowers

Figure 4.27 *Wisteria sinensis*, Beijing type, closer view.

(Biyunsi), Prince Gong's Mansion (Gongwangfu), Zhongshan Park, the Imperial Garden in the Forbidden City, Behai Park and the Summer Palace. Some of these appeared to be old plants, others to have been recently planted. While no two appeared identical, all resembled each other in general characteristics. They also appeared similar to the plant shown in bloom in Osvald Sirén's photograph taken in 1922 of the twin pavilions, Zhonghai, Beijing (figure 4.16). This is the only photograph I have come across of any wisteria in bloom in northern China. No white or pink variants were seen, not that this is to say they do not exist.

As with the southern form, it would certainly be worth introducing both light and dark selections with long racemes to gardens elsewhere. It may well prove that these types exhibit greater cold-hardiness than those from further south.

CULTIVARS

Various cultivar names occur in the literature and these are discussed below. In addition it seems that the form introduced to England from Guangzhou in 1816 and cultivated so widely should now be regarded as a cultivar, for which the name 'Consequa' is suggested.

'Alba'   Figures 4.28, 4.29

As for species seen south of the Yangtze, except rachis of raceme 20–35 cm with 55–85 flowers; deciduous bracts pale green; pedicels 2.0–2.5 cm, pale yellowish green; calyx green and white; standard 2.0–2.2 cm broad, pubescence at the top inside more extensive than in 'Consequa', rear glabrous except around the claw, blotch yellow-green, extending to about one-third of its height; wings and keel white; scent faint; legumes 5.8–16.5 cm, frequently produced, with 1–4 seeds, pinkish tan, heavily spotted and mottled with black. Summer flowers with the calyx suffused violet except at the lobes, darkest towards the pedicel. Autumn colour lemon yellow, quite good.

Apart from the colour and its longer racemes, this variant differs from the coloured cultivars in that the weakness of the pedicels allows the flowers to hang down close to the rachis, giving the racemes a narrow appearance. Well-grown it can be a charming plant, though the flowers present a slightly off-white effect.

It was introduced to England by Robert Fortune as described earlier in this chapter. It is not known to have been introduced subsequently and it seems probable that all plants with this name are descended from his introduction. After it flowered in the Horticultural Society's garden, it was described as *W. sinensis alba* by Lindley (1849), who wrote that apart from the colour 'it differs in no other respect from the lilac kind, and is much less handsome; but when plentiful it may produce a pretty effect by being inarched upon the branches of the latter.' I wonder whether anyone tried it, considering that his judgment of it was unjustifiably harsh. This, however, did not seem to impede its introduction to other parts of the world. In Australia, for instance, it was listed by Joseph Harrison's South Yarra Nurseries, Melbourne, in 1865.

Its subsequent nomenclatural history can be gleaned from Rehder (1949) who, along with Wilson (1916), described it as *W. sinensis* f. *alba* (Lindl.) Rehd. & Wils. There seems, however, no justification for according it any botanical status and it should be regarded merely as a cultivar. In Japan it is known as 'Shirobana Shina Fuji' ('White-flowered Chinese Wisteria').

'Alba Improved'

See 'Jako'.

'Alba Plena'

See *W. brachybotrys* 'Shiro Kapitan'.

Figure 4.28   *Wisteria sinensis* 'Alba'

Figure 4.29   *Wisteria sinensis* 'Alba'

'Amethyst'   Figure 4.30

Young foliage deep bronze. Flowers 25–40 on a rachis 12–18 cm long, tinged purple where exposed to sunlight; floral bracts purplish; pedicels green, purple towards the calyx; standard reddish violet, to 2.5 cm broad, pubescent at the top inside and around the claw outside, the blotch yellow, edged white; wings and keel darker; scent strong. Autumn colour poor.

This vigorous selection is offered in New Zealand. Its flowers are the most strongly scented of all the wisterias I have encountered, are a darker more reddish violet than those of 'Consequa', and are borne in shorter, fewer flowered racemes. It is an excellent wisteria and sufficiently distinct to warrant general cultivation.

Figure 4.30   *Wisteria sinensis* 'Amethyst'

'Black Dragon'

See 'Plena' and *W. floribunda* 'Royal Purple'.

'Blue Sapphire'

Similar to 'Consequa', but considered to be a superior form. Originated in New Zealand.

'Caroline'

'Caroline', a cultivar which is commercially available and has received frequent mention in recent years, often seems to find itself listed under *W. sinensis*. However, as it twines clockwise, has leaves with 13–15 leaflets and comparatively small flowers, it must be either a form of *W. floribunda* or a hybrid. Hence it is described in chapter 6 along with hybrids and wisterias of unknown provenance.

'Consequa'   Figure 4.31

Properly controlled, this is one of the great garden plants of all time. In order to distinguish it from other variants, it is proposed, in view of its history, that the form originally introduced to England be called 'Consequa', the anglicised version of the name of the Chinese merchant from whose garden it apparently came. As mentioned earlier in this chapter, it seems that the majority of plants of *W. sinensis* in cultivation outside China are this clone.

As it happens J. C. Loudon chose to give the species the name *W. consequana* on this account in 1830 (Rehder 1949), but since it had already been validly named *W. sinensis*, this name has been reduced to synonymy. There is, however, no reason for avoiding 'Consequa' as a cultivar name for the plant described as follows.

Young foliage bronze. Flowers soft blue-violet, the wings and keel darker than the standard, appearing with the leaves in racemes of 48–83; deciduous bracts small, pale green, tinged violet; rachis green, 16–22 cm, occasionally up

Figure 4.31 *Wisteria sinensis* 'Consequa'

to 33 cm; pedicels mauve, 1.5–2.2 cm; calyx violet; scent sweet; standard 2.2–2.5 cm broad, pubescent at the top inside, rear glabrous except for a few hairs around the claw, blotch extending to about half its height, yellow below, white above; legume small, usually with only one or two seeds, rarely produced in cultivation in most places. Autumn colour poor. Summer flowers darker and more reddish violet, produced abundantly in some seasons.

'Cooke's Special'

A seedling of similar colour to 'Consequa', introduced by the L. E. Cooke Co., Visalia, California. Most floriferous and reported to have spring racemes up to 50 cm long and to continue to produce shorter racemes throughout the summer. Obviously a good form.

'Flore Pleno'

See 'Plena'.

'Fuiri'

Kawarada (1985) mentions 'Fuiri Shina Fuji' ('Chinese Wisteria with Spots on the Leaves') but gives no evidence of its actual existence. Perhaps it is, or was, a variegated form.

'Jako'   **Figure 4.32**

Very similar to 'Alba' but strongly scented and with floral bracts sometimes edged mauve in strong light. Autumn colour poor.

'Jako' is the Japanese word for musk, and has sometimes been given as 'Jakoh', translated as 'Reindeer' or sold as 'Alba Improved'. It is also known in Japan as 'Nioi Fuji' ('Fragrant Wisteria'). So far I have not seen it in any nursery catalogue prior to 1930. However it may be what was listed among the 'Novelties and Rare Plants' in the catalogue of the Yokohama Nursery Company for 1905 as 'Fragrant Wistaria (Wistaria multijuga white)'. Other Japanese nurseries have listed '*W. multijuga praecox odorata alba*' (for example, Chugai Nursery Company 1959–60). No such names as these appear to be used in Japan at present and, since plants bought recently from there as *W. floribunda* 'Fragrantissima' have turned out to be 'Jako', it seems probable that these earlier listings under *W. multijuga* were this cultivar. Likewise the plant listed by Wohlert (1937) as '*W. floribunda praecox*—White' and described as 'very fragrant' is likely to have been the same. And the cultivar listed in Chapter 5 as *W. floribunda* 'Ivory Tower' may ultimately also prove to be 'Jako' (see page 90). Whatever the truth of all this may be, it seems clear that 'Jako' reached the rest of the world from Japan, but whether it was raised there or imported from China is unknown.

I saw only three wisteria plants with white flowers when in China in 1994. What appeared to be a very old vine in the Yu Yuan, Shanghai, looked to be identical with 'Alba'. Younger plants

Figure 4.32   *Wisteria sinensis* 'Jako'

(figure 4.21) at Zhuo Zheng Yuan, Suzhou, and Huanglongsi, Hangzhou, had strongly scented flowers and appeared identical with 'Jako'. Whether these were of Chinese or Japanese origin I do not know.

'Larry's White'

This cultivar produces 20–25 cm racemes of scented white flowers. It was obtained from Larry Poole of Forest Hill, Louisiana, by the Louisiana Nursery and named for him. It is apparently most prolific in bloom, small plants in pots being loaded down with flowers. The leaves usually have 11 leaflets. I have not been able to compare it with 'Alba' and 'Jako', and thus am unable to say whether it differs from these cultivars in botanical detail.

'Nioi Fuji'

See 'Jako'.

'Oosthoek's Variety'

See 'Prolific'.

'Plena'

A supposed double form, though I have so far found no evidence that such a cultivar exists, even though a double form or forms might be expected to occur. Other names given to supposed double forms include *W. sinensis flore pleno,* 'Black Dragon' and, in Japan, 'Yae Shina Fuji' ('Double Chinese Wisteria') or 'Yaezaki Shina Fuji' ('Double-flowering Chinese Wisteria').

The phenomenon of doubling usually involves a mutation leading to the development of petals instead of stamens, and this has certainly occurred in *W. floribunda.* While I can't say that double forms of *W. sinensis* do not exist, all plants I have examined so far bearing any of the above names have turned out to be the double form of *W. floribunda.*

There are several possible grounds for confusion. Firstly the double form of *W. floribunda* was first described by Carrière (1878) as *W. sinensis flore pleno.* Its Japanese name is 'Yae Kokuryu', which translates as 'Double Black Dragon'. Not only this but there is another form of *W. floribunda* called 'Hitoe Kokuryu', 'Single Black Dragon'. So the name 'Black Dragon' should be avoided anyway if a double form of *W. sinensis* does in fact exist.

'Praecox'

See *W. floribunda* 'Domino'.

'Prematura'

See *W. floribunda* 'Domino'.

'Prematura Alba'

See *W. brachybotrys* 'Shiro Kapitan'.

'Prolific'

Also known as 'Oosthoek's Variety', this cultivar was originally described by Gootendorst (1968) as having racemes 25 cm long, compared to 20–25 cm in the typical form. The illustration accompanying the description shows this to be the case, 'Prolific' having more flowers per raceme. Those wishing to obtain this cultivar should certainly see it in bloom first, as the only plants I have seen with this name were a short-racemed form of *W. floribunda.*

'Purpurea'

Plants are sometimes offered with this name simply to distinguish them from the white forms. It seems likely that they are usually 'Consequa'.

'Reindeer'

See 'Jako'.

'Rosea'

As with 'Plena', I have so far found no evidence that a pink cultivar exists. In many plants producing flowers with blue or violet pigments, as well as albino forms variants often appear with pink flowers. Canterbury Bells, hyacinths, bluebells and African Violets are but few of many well-known examples. Hence it seems not unlikely that, as has happened with *W. brachybotrys* and *W. floribunda,* there would be found a variant of *W. sinensis* with pink flowers. In fact just such a plant is listed by European and American nurseries as 'Rosea'. The Japanese list it as 'Usubeni', which means 'pale pink' or 'somewhat pink', or 'Usubeni Shina Fuji' ('Pale Pink Chinese Wisteria') and report it to have arisen in the United States (Kawarada 1985; Uehara 1961). All plants I have acquired so far as *W. sinensis* 'Rosea' have been pink forms of *W. floribunda,* and I have not as yet seen a pink *W. sinensis* anywhere. And I would have thought, in view of the popularity of *W. sinensis,* that if a pink form existed it would by now be widely promoted and planted. If a pink form does exist in cultivation, then perhaps it will soon become widely available. If it does not, then it is to be hoped such a plant will soon arise or be found.

'Shirobana Shina Fuji'

See 'Alba'

'Shirobana Yae Shina Fuji'

See *W. brachybotrys* 'Shiro Kapitan'.

'Sierra Madre'

The name 'Sierra Madre' was given to plants listed as a cultivar of *W. sinensis* propagated from the giant wisteria at the home of Mr and Mrs H. T. Fennel at Scenic Point, Sierra Madre ('Wistaria Town'), California. Apparently the specimen was planted in 1893 and was 90 m long altogether, being trained right around the house. In 1924 no fewer than 30 000 visitors saw it in full bloom (*Gardeners' Chronicle* 1925).

It was described by Wyman (1961) as having 'clusters eight inches [about 20 cm]; excellent fragrance; 13 leaflets; flower standard whitish, wings and keel sea lavender violet 637/1; merely propagated from a vine at Sierra Madre, California, that has been given wide publicity. This may be a hybrid.' In view of this last comment, its having leaves with 13 leaflets and its direction of twining not being recorded, its identity remains uncertain. As far as I know it is no longer offered by nurseries.

'Usubeni', 'Usubeni Shina Fuji'

See 'Rosea'.

'Yae Shina Fuji', 'Yaezaki', 'Yaezaki Shina Fuji'

See 'Plena'.

OTHER CULTIVARS

While I can vouch for the information given above, there are other names listed from time to time by nurserys and in the gardening literature as cultivars of this species for which accurate descriptions have not been obtained. If or in what way they differ from those described above I do not know. Such plants are usually described as 'selected forms'.

Also, if it has not happened already (see 'Fuiri' above), a variant or variants with variegated foliage might well turn up, as might a dwarf form. In this regard W. B. Clarke's nursery in San Jose, California, listed *W. sinensis* 'Nankingensis' in the 1930s, stating that it had very small leaves, was practically a dwarf, and had not bloomed yet. This does not seem to have been heard of since and was probably the dwarf form of *Millettia japonica* described in chapter 7.

As is clear from the list of cultivar names already given, a number rightfully belong in other species. To these must be added 'Beni Fugi', a cultivar described as having long pendulous racemes and listed under *W. sinensis* in the past by Duncan and Davies of New Plymouth, New Zealand, and which seems likely to have belonged in *W. floribunda* (see chapter 5).

Other Chinese species

Wisterias collected in China have been given various names but most of these are now considered to be synonyms of *W. sinensis*. However, names which, as far as I am aware, have not been reduced to synonymy are *W. brevidentata* Rehd., *W. praecox* Hand. Mazz. and *W. villosa* Rehd. There may be others.

W. brevidentata Rehd.

Rehder (1926b) described this from a specimen collected early this century by the Jesuit missionary E. E. Maire from gardens at Dongchuan, Yunnan, at 2500 m, and included in the species were specimens collected in Fuzhou, Fujian, on 8 and 9 April 1923 (Herbarium of the University of Amoy, nos. 1265 and 1291).

It is described as having small leaves with 9–13 leaflets, racemes 10–18 cm with violet flowers, the standard 1.5 cm, borne on pedicels 6–12 mm long. Again I have not seen the specimens on which this description is based, but at Kew there is a specimen collected at Fuzhou on 9 April 1923, marked no. 1291 and labelled W. brevidentata. This has white flowers in a many-flowered raceme 35 cm long and leaves with 13–15 leaflets.

It is strange that a specimen apparently collected in Fuzhou on the same day and with the same number should be so different from Rehder's description, having much longer racemes, white flowers and larger leaves with 13–15 leaflets. These features, together with its relatively small flowers suggest it might more satisfactorily be placed in W. floribunda.

To add to the confusion, there is another specimen at Kew labelled W. brevidentata, also from Fuzhou, marked no. 1323, described as a tree 4 m, flowers white. This has racemes about 12 cm long with approximately 30 flowers and leaves with 11 leaflets. Apart from the flower colour it roughly fits Rehder's description but it looks like a small weak form of W. sinensis.

Again one would have to see the specimens listed by Rehder to unravel all this. If the type specimen agrees with Rehder's description then perhaps it might merely be considered a variant of W. sinensis. And since it was being grown at 2500 m, this may have had an effect on its appearance.

W. praecox Hand.-Mazz.

This was described by the Austrian botanist Heinrich von Handel-Mazzetti (1921) from specimens he collected at low altitudes near Changsha, Hunan, in April 1918, and another collected by Ernest Wilson in western Hubei in 1901.

Handel-Mazzetti describes it as having leaves with 9–13 leaflets, racemes 12–16 cm with about 30 flowers, pedicels 1.2–1.7 cm, the flowers deep rose or reddish violet, the standard 2.2 cm in diameter. He claimed it to be close to W. venusta (W. brachybotrys 'Shiro Kapitan'), which differs in its longer pedicels, white flowers appearing with the leaves, and with more-pointed, indumented leaflets, and to W. sinensis and W. floribunda, which are more glabrous and with flowers of a different colour and further apart.

The description strongly suggests a short-racemed form of W. sinensis with reddish violet flowers, similar to specimens seen both in cultivation and growing spontaneously in Shanghai, Jiangsu, Zhejiang and Anhui in April 1994, and to the short-racemed, reddish violet cultivar 'Amethyst' described above. Again a final decision awaits the re-examination of the original specimens.

W. villosa Rehd.

Rehder and Wilson (1916) included a fruiting specimen collected by F. N. Meyer in 1913 near Qinhuangdao, Hebei, in their new species W. venusta, otherwise known only from Japan. Later Rehder (1926b) changed his mind and placed this specimen, along with others from northern China, in yet another new species, W. villosa. Included in the synonymy were W. chinensis as recorded from northern China by the Russian botanist Alexander von Bunge, and W. brachybotrys as recorded from Beijing by Forbes and Hemsley (1887). According to Bretschneider (1898), von Bunge arrived in Beijing in November 1830 and

collected specimens in April, May and June of 1831 before returning to Russia in July.

The type specimen is given as having been collected at the 'Temple of Sleeping Buddha, Wo-fu-ssu, western hills near Peking. *Ralph G. Mills, July 25, 1923* (type).' The other specimens listed were collected in September and October, so it seems likely that they do not bear flowers.

A cursory examination of flowering specimens from northern China in the herbarium at Kew has shown them to be similar to one another, whether attributed to *W. sinensis* or *W. villosa*. They had been collected in the first few days of May in various years. Likewise in late April 1994 I was able to examine many wisterias in bloom in and near Beijing, including an old vine in the courtyard of the Temple of the Sleeping Buddha (Wofosi), which may well be the plant from which Mills's specimen came (figure 4.33). I have not seen his specimen but Rehder's description fits the present plant there and accommodates all other wisterias seen during the same visit to Beijing.

In the comments accompanying his description Rehder said that *W. villosa* is 'closely related to *W. sinensis* Sweet which differs chiefly in its silky straight less dense pubescence more or less yellowish and lustrous on young leaves and disappearing almost entirely at maturity; the leaves usually only half-grown at flowering time and the leaflets cuneate or broad-cuneate at the base; the tomentum of the fruit which is usually shorter and has fewer seeds is fulvous'.

I have not noticed the pubescence on the young leaves of *W. sinensis* to be yellowish, nor to disappear almost entirely at maturity, since it remains on and sometimes near the veins beneath. While it may be that the pubescence is more per-sistent on the undersurface in the Beijing specimens and others from northern China, this does not seem to me to be an important difference.

Likewise the statement that *W. sinensis* differs in the leaves being only half-grown at flowering time suggests that *W. villosa* does not bloom until the leaves are fully expanded. This, however, is likely to be so on any specimen collected as late as 25 July, as presumably such a specimen would be one of the occasional racemes produced in summer terminally on a shoot of the current season, long after the main flowering.

Also, if the leaflets of *W. sinensis* are described as cuneate (wedge-shaped) or broad-cuneate at the base, it is hard to see how this differs markedly from a broadly cuneate or rounded base as given for *W. villosa*. And as for the differences in the fruits and the number of seeds, one would have to see the full range of variation in *W. sinensis* before drawing any conclusions. Since there is enormous variation within *W. floribunda* in this regard it would not be surprising to find that a similar situation exists in *W. sinensis*.

It would be necessary to re-examine the specimens listed by Rehder to be certain that they are not significantly different from the wisterias now in cultivation in and around Beijing, however there seems to be no reason at present for not following Chinese botanists in considering these latter to be forms of *W. sinensis*. For this reason they were described as such earlier in this chapter.

All in all it is clear that there is considerable variation within *Wisteria* as it occurs both in cultivation and in the wild in China. Whether botanists will eventually regard Chinese wisterias as belonging to one variable species or a number of similar but separate species remains to be seen.

Figure 4.33
Wisteria sinensis
at Wofosi, Beijing

CHAPTER   5

Japanese Wisterias

More is known and recorded about the Japanese wisteria species than all the others put together. These splendid plants have been esteemed by the Japanese for hundreds of years, have given rise to numerous cultivars and feature prominently in Japanese art and literature.

The two species which are widely cultivated are *W. brachybotrys* and *W. floribunda*. Since the latter is the better known, it will be described first.

W. floribunda (Willd.) DC.

JAPANESE WISTERIA, FUJI, NODA FUJI

Perhaps because it requires a little more care in its training and pruning to give its best, *W. floribunda* has not generally been as popular outside Japan as *W. sinensis*. If anything, however, it is even more decorative. With its many-flowered racemes it remains in bloom longer, its growth habit is more graceful, the disposition of its blossoms and foliage more elegant, and its autumn colour more effective. Well I think so anyway.

These characteristics have long appealed to the Japanese. The earliest written reference to it appears to be in the *Kojiki* ('Records of Ancient Matters'), compiled from oral tradition in 712, which includes myths, legends and historical accounts of the Imperial Court from the earliest days of its creation up to the reign of the Empress Suiko (628). In the English translation (Philippi 1969) it is related that, during the reign of the Emperor Ojin, there was a beautiful maiden called Idusi-Wotome, whom everyone

Figure 5.1   *Wisteria floribunda* 'Shiro Noda', a much admired Japanese cultivar

Figure 5.2 Wisteria crest, Kasuga Shrine, Nara

wanted to marry but no one could persuade to do so, including the elder of two brothers, both deities. This elder brother then wagered that if the younger could win her then he would hand over to him a variety of valuable objects. Their mother then took wisteria vines and wove them, in one night, into a jacket, trousers, stockings and shoes. She also made a bow and arrows. Dressing the younger brother in these clothes, she had him take the bow and arrows and go to the maiden's house, whereupon the clothes and the bow and arrows turned into wisteria blossoms. He hung up his bow and arrows in the maiden's privy and she, thinking the blossoms strange took them with her. He followed her into the house and, as the translator puts it, immediately they had conjugal relations. After a child was born he said to his elder brother 'I have won Idusi-Wotome'. The elder brother was not pleased by this news and failed to honour the bet, which, as invariably happens in tales of this sort, led to further complexities.

Wisteria is mentioned several times in the *Manyoshu,* an anthology of poems compiled about 759 AD, both for its beauty and for the use of its bark for weaving cloth. Included is one poem which indicates that it was being cultivated by this time. This is number 1471 in volume 8, by Akahito Yamabe, which has been translated (Suga 1991) as follows:

The wistaria
I planted in my garden
As a token of love
Is now waving its clusters
Of gorgeous purple flowers.

It had certainly become a popular plant by the Heian Period (794–1185) and is mentioned by Murasaki Shikibu (10th & 11th centuries) in her famous novel *The Tale of Genji.* There are written references from this period to the holding of garden parties to admire wisteria flowers (Miyazawa 1940). And the Fujiwara family, who came to power at this time, did so, it is claimed, as the result of a plot hatched in a wisteria arbour. Hence the name they adopted. The Kasuga Shrine at Nara, which the Fujiwaras patronised, has as its crest a stylised wisteria (figure 5.2).

According to Miyazawa there was a famous wisteria-viewing site at Fuji-no-miya ('Wisteria Shrine') at a village called Noda, in an area which has now become part of Osaka. This shrine, with its wisteria, was visited by members of the Fujiwara clan who composed poems in its honour and established there the god Kasuga-myojin, from whom they claimed descent. On account of its fame it was later visited by one of the Ashikaga shoguns, who gave the shrine a statue of Benten, the Chinese Goddess of Mercy, and in the 1590s by Toyotomi Hideyoshi, who drank tea there and admired the flowers. According to Miyazawa, there is a publication of the late seventeenth century in which the size, age and beauty of the wisteria at Noda is described, and for a long time the tradition of offering poems and making wishes was observed. During the Edo period (1600–1853) there were many such famous wisteria-viewing sites, particularly in and near Kyoto and Edo (now Tokyo) (Makino et al. 1955).

In addition to this, wisteria became a favourite decorative motif as well as being represented in paintings, particularly from the early seven-teenth century on. Exquisite examples (figure 5.3) can be seen in art galleries and as decorations on walls and screens in famous old buildings. At Nishi Honganji in Kyoto, for example, there is a room, which probably dates from the late six-teenth century, overlooking the Tiger Glen Garden and decorated entirely with paintings depicting several variants.

Miyazawa notes that a book called *Hanafu* ('Flower Calendar'), published about 1695 describes methods of growing wisterias and lists several varieties including a white one and 'Yama Fuji' (*W. brachybotrys*). However, while there are many references to wisteria in Japanese classical literature, according to Kawarada (1985) none of the early ones gives any indication of its being grown over a pergola, now the most popular and effective way of growing the plant. He and others report that there is a reference which says that the Muromachi shogun, Ashikaga Yoshimasa, planted a white wisteria in 1461, trained it along the roof of his house, and enjoyed admiring the flowers six years later.

Kawarada suggests that Yoshimasa's treatment of his white wisteria may have been the forerunner of the pergola method. Anyway Miyazawa says that growing wisterias on pergolas became well established in the Genroku Period (1688–1703) and Kawarada records that the first known written reference to a wisteria pergola ('fujidana', literally 'wisteria shelf') is dated 1701. This reports that an old wisteria was growing on a pergola at the famous shrine in Noda, Osaka.

Where space allows, growing the plant over a pergola is undoubtedly one of the most effective ways of displaying the long pendulous racemes (figures 5.4–5.5). It is also frequently trained as a standard or as a shrub, with the branches usually supported by wooden props (figure 5.6), and as a bonsai (figure 5.7). Also in

Figure 5.3 Wisteria scroll, painted on silk by Hon'ami Koho (1601–82) (Tokyo National Museum)

Figure 5.4   Wisteria at Ushijima, 6 May 1914 (E. H. Wilson)

Figure 5.5   Wisteria at Ushijima, 8 May 1991

Figure 5.6 Wisteria in Japan trained as a shrub supported by wooden props

Figure 5.7 *Wisteria floribunda* 'Shiro Noda' as bonsai, Kamata, 12 May 1914 (E. H. Wilson)

the Tohoku area, according to Kawarada (1985), you can see old houses enclosed by wisteria hedges shaped like a dragon swimming.

Although the original name for *W. floribunda* is 'Fuji', it now seems commonly to be called 'Noda Fuji' to distinguish it from other wisterias. Boehmer (1903), for instance, says that the variety grown at the Kameido Shrine in Tokyo is called Noda Fuji, and goes on to describe several kinds of Noda Fuji growing in his nursery in Yokohama. Likewise Florence Du Cane (1908) writes 'Noda in the province of Settsu is also celebrated for its wisteria, and a special variety has been named after the place.'

In view of all this, and since the plant occurs wild throughout the whole of Japan south of Hokkaido, it may seem surprising that it was not introduced to cultivation elsewhere, except perhaps China, until the middle of the nineteenth century. But it must be remembered that Japan was no more welcoming to foreigners than was China. In fact Japan was closed to foreigners from 1638 to 1858 and the Japanese themselves were forbidden to travel abroad during this period.

In spite of these strictures the Dutch, who unlike the Spanish and Portuguese, appeared to be in no rush to convert the populace to Christianity, were allowed to maintain a trading station on Deshima, a small artificial island in Nagasaki harbour. It is largely through the work of three European physicians who worked for the Dutch East India Company on Deshima that any knowledge of Japanese botany and horticulture reached the outside world at all during this period.

Engelbert Kaempfer, a German physician and botanist, was there from 1690 to 1692. Although confined to the island for most of his stay, he accumulated specimens and information about Japanese plants and made drawings of them. This knowledge was much increased by his being allowed to travel to Edo (Tokyo) in 1691 and 1692, when the Dutch superintendent went there to pay his annual respects to the Tokugawa shogun. On his return to Europe he described many Japanese plants in his *Amoenitatum Exoticarum* (1712). In this he lists two wisterias, the ordinary 'Too or Fudsi' (now *W. floribunda*) and 'Jamma Fudsi' (now *W. brachybotrys*). He records that the former may have flowers either purple or white.

In a French version of his work, published posthumously (1736), there is an extended lyrical passage in which he describes the Japanese Wisteria as a vigorous climber covering arbours and bowers and producing abundant racemes, one to one-and-a-half handspans in length, which are followed by pods containing black beans, though this occurs rarely. He goes on to say that one finds at Osaka and elsewhere large areas completely covered by a single plant or by two or three. He notes that people put the dregs of sake around the base of the plant to fertilise it and that this results in the plant producing racemes three or four handspans long. He records, too, that visitors pay to see such large vines, where one may encounter a benevolent spirit, and that they write poems in honour of the goddess believed to preside in these beautiful places. Again he states that the flowers are either all white or all purple. And his description strongly suggests that he may have visited the famous vine at Fuji-no-miya.

Over eighty years later Linnaeus's pupil, Carl Thunberg, took up the position of physician on Deshima from 1775 to 1778. On his return to Sweden he too published a description of this wisteria, calling it *Dolichos polystachyos* in his *Flora Japonica* (1784).

Its subsequent nomenclatural history may be gleaned from Rehder (1949) as follows. It appears that in 1782 the Dutch botanist Martin Houttyn had named it *Dolichos polystachios*, presumably on the basis of a specimen of Thunberg's, and Thunberg in his later publication altered the spelling.

However this name had been used earlier by Linnaeus for a different plant, so Willdenow (1800) gave Thunberg's plant the name *Glycine floribunda*. It was ultimately transferred to the genus *Wisteria* by De Candolle (1825) and hence its correct name is now *W. floribunda* (Willd.) DC.

Meanwhile further observations were being made in Japan by Phillip von Siebold, who went to Deshima in 1823 and who, like his predecessors, was able to journey to the capital, Edo. Eventually he fell foul of the Tokugawa Shogunate and was expelled in December 1828. However, with the aid of his students he was able to send herbarium specimens and living plants back to Europe.

Those plants which survived the journey were introduced to Ghent on his return there in 1830 but, with the struggle for Belgian independence, he was forced to flee and his collection was confiscated and distributed among the city's nurserymen. When peace was restored he established a Jardin d'Acclimatization at Leiden and later, with C. L. Blume, he founded a society to introduce Japanese plants to Europe. This became commercialised into the firm of Siebold and Company, which received a steady flow of plants over the years (Huxley, Griffiths & Levy 1992).

Also Siebold, together with J. G. Zuccarini, wrote a large illustrated *Flora Japonica* (1835–41), and in this *W. floribunda* is described and illustrated under the names *W. chinensis* and *W. sinensis*, presumably because they assumed it to belong to that Chinese species. Apparently Siebold had seen it only as a cultivated plant in Japan. He recorded that there were several varieties, varying in length of raceme and in colour, the variety with purple flowers being known as 'Beni-fudsi' and the white one as 'Siro-fudsi'.

Also described are arbours, covered ways and pergolas from which numerous racemes, often a metre long, hung down under which, in April and

May, all classes of society gathered to drink sake and dance or sing to the accompaniment of instruments. As Kaempfer had recorded earlier, it is noted that they wrote poems, and that they attached them, written on strips of paper, to the most beautiful racemes.

Siebold also recorded that Japanese literature is rich in poems written in honour of 'Fudsi', symbol of spring, and that valuable pictures of this plant in bloom are preserved in galleries. Also, during a journey to Edo, he saw little messages of all colours attached to the racemes of a wisteria in the courtyard of a temple, and was told that young people attached them, taking the vigour of the development of these racemes as an omen of the outcome of their future marriages.

It seems that *W. floribunda* was not among the plants introduced to Ghent in 1830. Various authors (Rehder & Wilson 1916; Wilson 1916; Rehder 1927; Wyman 1969; McMillan Browse 1984; Nédélec 1992) have stated that it was introduced about this time, but this view is based upon what I believe to be Wilson's (1916) mistaken assumption that the plant introduced, Siebold's and Zuccarini's *W. brachybotrys*, was merely a short-racemed form of *W. floribunda*. There seems to be no evidence that *W. floribunda* was introduced at this time. Wilson himself (1916) said that it appeared not to have been known in gardens until much later. In view of its horticultural appeal this in itself seems odd.

Bean (1980) says that it was introduced, in one or more of its cultivated forms, to Holland by Siebold in 1856, which seems more likely, and that it appears to have attracted little notice at first, perhaps because it was slow to flower or was wrongly pruned.

The first illustration of flowers from a plant in cultivation in Europe appears to be that in the *Flore des Serres* (Houtte 1873) as *W. multijuga*. The name *multijuga* means 'many yoked together' in

allusion to the many-flowered racemes. In the accompanying note Louis van Houtte says it bears racemes twice as long as shown in the plate, so there can be little doubt that this was the cultivar now known as 'Macrobotrys'. A plant obtained from van Houtte was susequently illustrated in *Curtis's Botanical Magazine* (Hooker 1897).

Other cultivars arrived later, probably most of them being obtained from nurseries in Japan. For instance Cyril Ward (1912), describing Royal Gardens in Britain early this century, says that at Bagshot Park 'the walls are covered with good forms of the mauve and white wistaria in alternate colours, the original plants having been brought from Japan by Their Royal Highnesses the Duke and Duchess of Connaught in 1888. They never fail to flower in their season with the greatest possible freedom.' His description is accompanied by a reproduction of his own watercolour of the wisteria pergola at Bagshot Park and the 'exquisitely furnished Japanese house' presented to Prince Arthur of Connaught by the Japanese government.

Kaempfer (1712, 1736), Siebold (1835–41), Fortune (1863) and Du Cane (1908) make no mention of cultivars with double flowers or colours other than purple or white, though they did note that there was variation in the length of the racemes produced. However Boehmer (1903) listed purple, lavender, white and double forms and the Yokohama Nursery Company had a pale pink form at least as early as 1905. Other cultivars were listed by Japanese nurseries from time to time thereafter and thus found their way to the rest of the world.

After 1858, when Japan became accessible to foreign visitors once more, there are various descriptions of the beauty of the wisterias there. Robert Fortune (1863), for instance, went to see a famous vine near Tokyo on 20 May 1861, and reported that 'it measured, at three feet [0.9 m]

Figure 5.8 Wisteria at Kameido by Ella Du Cane (from *Flowers and Gardens of Japan*, 1908)

from the ground, seven feet [2.1 m] in circumference, and covered a space of trellis-work sixty feet by one hundred and two feet [about 18 m × 31 m]. The trellis was about eight feet [2.4 m] in height, and many thousands of the racemes of the glycine hung down nearly half-way to the ground. One of them, which I measured, was three feet six inches [1.06 m] in length. The thousands of long drooping lilac racemes had a most extraordinary and beautiful appearance. People came from far and near to see the tree the time it remained in bloom; and as it was in the garden of a public tea-house, it brought an extensive custom to the proprietor. The tables and benches were arranged under its shade, which at the time of our visit were well occupied with travellers and visitors, all sipping and enjoying the grateful and invigorating beverage. As the day was cloudless, and the sun's rays powerful, we were not slow to imitate the example they set before us, so we

sipped our tea, smoked a cigar, and admired this beautiful specimen of the vegetable kingdom.'

Perhaps Fortune's visit was a little early in the day for the sake mentioned by Kaempfer and Siebold, though some forty years on, Florence Du Cane (1908), while sitting under the famous wisteria at Kameido, ordered a cup so that she might empty some on the roots in the hope of contributing to its great size and beauty. She gives an evocative account of the scene in her book *The Flowers and Gardens of Japan*, which is illustrated with reproductions of Ella Du Cane's watercolours, seven of which depict wisterias, including those at Kameido (figure 5.8). This celebrated wisteria-viewing site had been depicted by others before her, including Hiroshige, whose woodblock print forms one of his *One Hundred Views of Edo* (figure 5.9).

Florence Du Cane also comments 'Very lovely is the scene at Kashukabe, where another famous wistaria grows. The vine is said to be some 500 years old, its pendant clusters over 50 inches [about 1.3 m] long and growing over trellises covering a space of 4000 feet [some 1200 m].'

Ernest Wilson (1916) photographed this plant (figure 5.4) in 1914 and measured a raceme 1.64 m long. And Alice Coats (1964) notes that 'Mr Collingwood Ingram has described the famous specimen at Ushijima near Kasukaba, supposed to have been planted by the priest Kobo Daishi; in 1920 this venerable plant had a trunk 32 feet [9.75 m] in circumference, and covered a trellis approximately 400 square yards [about 335 m²] in extent with upwards of 80,000 close hung trusses of flowers.' It apparently survived the earthquake of 1923 and in 1929 was visited by P. H. Dorsett (1935), who also photographed

it and measured racemes up to 1.2 m long (figure 5.10).

As far as wisteria-viewing goes things seem to have stayed much the same for centuries. The visitors still drink sake, along now with beer and the ubiquitous Coca Cola. And at the Kasuga Shrine in Nara you can still see messages or prayers tied to wisterias. People continue to go to the Kameido Shrine, now a short walk from Kameido station on the Tokyo suburban railway, and to Ushijima, the village near Kasukabe where the famous wisteria grows, close to both Fuji-no-Ushijima and Kasukabe stations.

Nowadays, according to the information on the back of the ticket (figure 5.11) admitting one to the Ushijima wisteria, the vine is more than 1200 years old, covers 700 m² of trellis and has

Figure 5.9   Wisteria at Kameido by Hiroshige (1797–1858)

Figure 5.10   Wisteria at Ushijima, 15 May 1929 (P. H. Dorsett)

特別天然記念物

牛 島 の 藤

● 入園保存料

大人…… 800 円

小供…… 400 円

埼玉県春日部市牛島７８６

☎ 048(752)2012

Figure 5.11 Entrance ticket to the wisteria at Ushijima

given rise to a number of trunks over an area of 10 m². It was listed as a Special Natural Item in 1928 and declared a National Treasure in 1955. Recent examination of this pergola shows it to be covered by two very old vines, one or other or both of which presumably constitute the National Treasure. Perhaps the second one arose long ago as a sucker from the roots of the first. Anyway its fame is reflected in the price of admission, 800 yen at the time of my visit, considerably more than that for any other horticultural display or garden.

As well as the Ushijima wisteria, Kawarada (1985) lists six others which have been declared National Treasures. These are Fujishima-no-fuji in Iwate prefecture, Yama-no-kami-no-fuji in Yamanashi prefecture, Yuya-no-naga-fuji in Shizuoka prefecture, Miyazaki-jingu-no-o-shira-fuji in Miyazaki prefecture, which Kawarada says is *W. sinensis*, Takimae- or Takizen-fudo in Miyagi prefecture and Kuroki-no-fuji (Sanshaku Fuji) in Fukuoka prefecture. In addition to these he mentions Jochinji-no-fuji in Ishikaya prefecture, which is not a National Treasure but which is another very large and famous plant. Further large old wisterias are listed by Uehara (1961), including Sanshoku Fuji (Three-coloured Wisteria) at the Hoe-ji temple, 300 years old and with purple, white and pink flowers.

Those wishing to see a collection of cultivars may easily do so in the Tokyo area at the Koishikawa Botanical Garden, Tokyo, the garden of the Shinshoji Temple, Narita, and the Jindai Botanical Park near Chofu. No doubt there are others further afield. At the Manyo Botanical Garden near the Kasuga Shrine, Nara, where are gathered together all the plants mentioned in the *Manyoshu*, it is planned to assemble as complete as possible a collection of wisterias.

Florence Du Cane (1908) is a mine of information about wisterias. She says that wisteria and tree peonies seem to be closely associated, as they flower at the same time and many gardens seem devoted to their combined culture (figure 5.12). And in addition to repeating the folklore concerning sake, she records that 'the young tender leaves of wistaria are sometimes eaten, and also used in place of tea; and the flowers themselves are used as food in some parts of China. The seeds baked in the fire have very much the same flavour as that of a chestnut.' No fear of poisoning here apparently (see previous chapter).

She continues: 'The bark is used for rope and sandals, and its branches are used, it is said, as cables, and also for bridge making, as it is supposed that there is nothing more durable than a wistaria bridge. Japanese antiquarians will tell you that in olden times, before carpenters' tools had been invented, the dwellings of the people in Japan were constructed of young trees with the bark left on, fastened together with ropes made of the tough shoots of wistaria, and thatched with the grass called *kava*.'

In a different vein she tells us that 'one of the most celebrated classical *No* dances of Japan has wistaria as its theme … The priest, who is a necessary part of any *No* dance, is the first to appear on the stage; he is supposed to reach Taka no Ura in the province of Ecchu, a place famous for wistaria, and here he meets a country girl who in a short time will reappear as the spirit of the wistaria; she entreats him to pray for her, so that through the virtue of his prayer her flower spirit may enter into Nirvana or Paradise; doubtless the spirit of the last flower of spring is not able to release herself from the world to attain Buddhistic perfection, so she hates to say her quick farewell to spring. Presently the flower spirit, arrayed in gorgeous purple brocade, dances her last spring dance, and then, after receiving the priest's repeated prayer, she will disappear with joy. So ends the *No* play, so full of emblematical meaning to the minds of the Japanese.'

DESCRIPTION

As with most species, *W. floribunda* (figure 5.13) exhibits considerable variation in the wild. The general description below is based on my own observations.

Vigorous deciduous climber, twining clockwise. Leaves up to 35 cm long, with 11–17 leaflets; leaflets ovate-elliptic to oblong, to 8 cm, pale green or bronze-green when young, sparsely pubescent above and below, the hairs usually longer

Figure 5.12 *Wisteria floribunda* 'Kuchibeni'
and tree peony 'Kokirin'

Figure 5.13 *Wisteria floribunda*
growing wild at Nikko

above than below, becoming almost glabrous except on the veins below. Inflorescence buds in winter pointed, 5–7 mm × 2.0–2.5 mm, outer two bracts dark reddish brown, pubescent only at the base outside, completely covering the inner bracts for most of the dormant season. Flowers usually violet in many-flowered racemes, appearing with the leaves, scented; deciduous floral bracts small, pubescent, usually tinged purple; rachis green, pubescent, frequently 30 cm or more in length; pedicels to 3 cm, pubescent, green, sometimes suffused purple; calyx pubescent, frequently purplish, lower three lobes prominent, pointed; standard 1.5–2.0 cm broad, auricled, with a yellow blotch extending to about half its height, pubescent at the top on its inner surface, outer surface glabrous or sparsely pubescent around the claw, sometimes with a few hairs extending up the mid-line; wings each with a short pointed auricle, apex rounded or with an obtuse point; keel elements each with a short rounded or obtusely pointed auricle, apex with an obtuse point; stamens 10, glabrous, 9 joined, 1 free; ovary pubescent, developing into a woody velutinous legume with 1–8 flattened seeds, brown, usually mottled and streaked with black (figure 5.14).

In relation to the scent, it is interesting to note that it is probably made up of many chemical components, as 120 volatile compounds have been isolated from the flowers (Watanabe et al. 1988).

While *W. floribunda* is generally known in Japan simply as 'Fuji' or 'Noda Fuji', Uehara (1961) also lists 'No Fuji' ('Wild Wisteria') and 'Maboshi Fuji' ('Loose-clustered Wisteria') among its names.

As mentioned earlier, it occurs wild throughout Japan south of Hokkaido, often along the banks of streams, and is widely cultivated. It also can be seen growing spontaneously in South Korea, again particularly on streambanks, roadsides and hillsides bordering ricefields. As it

seems to occur there largely in areas which have been subjected to human interference, it is impossible for me to say whether it is truly indigenous or has become naturalised. As well it is extensively cultivated in South Korea, apparently almost exclusively as seedling forms. In addition to being grown in parks and private gardens, it can be seen on pergolas in roadside rest areas and planted to grow over steep roadside banks, presumably to stabilise them. South Korea is the only country in which I have seen the plant used in this manner. Thus, in early May *W. floribunda* is particularly conspicuous in that country. The plant described as *W. koreana* Uyeki is apparently now considered to belong in *W. floribunda*.

Only in Seoul did I see Japanese cultivars and then only once, on a large pergola in the garden of the Toksugung Palace. Growing over this were old plants of 'Macrobotrys', 'Shiro Noda', 'Honbeni' and 'Violacea Plena'. Perhaps these had been planted during the Japanese occupation.

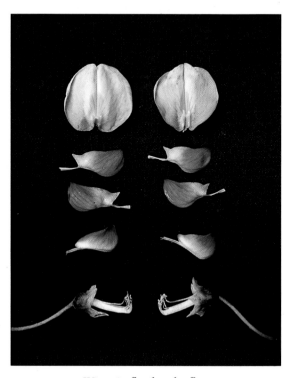

Figure 5.14 *Wisteria floribunda*, flower structure

CULTIVARS

Named cultivars have been known in Japan for hundreds of years and new ones continue to be introduced from time to time. Also, unlike *W. sinensis*, *W. floribunda* sets seed abundantly in cultivation, with the result that large numbers of seedlings have been raised in other parts of the world, many of which have proved to be attractive garden plants. A few of these have been named and distributed. Most of the named cultivars, however, are Japanese in origin. Some of these have been described in the past as botanical forms or varieties though only deserving of cultivar status.

With regard to the cultivar names, one of the sources of confusion has been the use of the Japanese word 'issai', which means 'one year old' and is used by Japanese growers to refer to cultivars which might be expected to bloom one year after grafting, or at least earlier than most others. Hence it is used in the sense of 'early maturing'. This has also resulted in distributors using such names as 'Praecox' and 'Prematura' for western markets, names which have sometimes been wrongly taken as indicating that these cultivars flower early in the season, when in fact this may not be so.

Those cultivars which have come to my notice are listed below, the descriptions, where given, focussing on differences from that already given for the wild type.

'Akabana'

See 'Honbeni'.

'Akebono'

See 'Kuchibeni'

'Alabama'

See 'Honbeni'.

'Alba'

See 'Shiro Noda'.

'Albomaculata'

See 'Nishiki'.

'Alborosea'

See 'Kuchibeni'.

'Arakawa'

The name means 'rough bark'. This cultivar develops rough, creviced bark from about the third year on and because of this is popular for bonsai in Japan. According to Kawarada (1985) its flowers are violet in racemes 20–30 cm long.

'Aranami'

A name encountered in Japan about which I have been unable to obtain any information.

'Asagi', 'Asagi Shibori'

According to Kawarada (1985) this is a very old cultivar with pale blue flowers in short racemes 15–20 cm long, used for bonsai. Some plants in the trade as 'Hichirimen' and 'Noda Issai' appear to be this. A plant I obtained under the latter name has pale flowers in racemes 12.5–18.5 cm long with 39–49 flowers, faint scent, pedicels green to 1.7 cm, and leaves with 13–15 leaflets. 'Asagi' means 'pale yellow' and 'shibori' means 'tie-dyed'. Presumably these names refer to the colour of the blotch on the standard petal.

'Beni Fuji'

This name appears from time to time in the literature and nursery catalogues. Since it merely means 'red wisteria' it seems sufficiently imprecise as to be overlooked. It is sometimes included as a synonym of 'Honbeni' (Tsukamoto 1984), which see.

'Black Dragon'

See 'Royal Purple' and 'Violacea Plena'.

'Botan Fuji'

See 'Violacea Plena'.

'Burford'

See Chapter 6.

'Carnea'

See 'Kuchibeni'.

'Caroline'

On the basis of its morphological characteristics this cultivar appears to be a form of W. floribunda. However, in view of the uncertainty surrounding its provenance and as it is often listed under W. sinensis, it is described in Chapter 6.

'Coelestina'

According to Bean (1980) this lavender blue cultivar was named by Sprenger, the Naples nurseryman, in 1911. It does not appear any longer to be available.

From Bean's reference under this name to a note by Boehmer (1903), one might infer that the pale lavender cultivar growing in the nursery of L. Boehmer and Company, Yokohama, and described in this note was imported and given this name by Sprenger. However I have not been able to confirm this.

'Domino' Figure 5.15

This cultivar was sent to Europe by Koichiro Wada, the renowned Japanese nurseryman, best known for introducing Rhododendron yakushimanum to the Western world. It was described by Grootendorst (1968) as having light lilac blue flowers in racemes 18–25 cm long, and leaves with 13–15 leaflets, pale green when young.

Plants fitting this description have appeared with the names 'Issai', 'Issai Fuji', 'Multijuga Praecox', 'Prematura', 'Praecox' and 'Domino'. Since 'Domino' is the only one of these which avoids ambiguity it seems wise to retain it for this cultivar, at least outside Japan. In Australia a plant listed as 'Izuzu' seems similar.

As I have seen it, 'Domino' has leaves with 11–15 leaflets, pale green when young, sometimes tinged with bronze. Racemes 15–22 cm long with 50–78 flowers; pedicels to 3 cm, pale green, suffused mauve where exposed to strong light; standard clear bluish violet, 1.6–1.8 cm broad, pubescent at the top on the inner surface and around the claw outside; wings and keel darker and more reddish; scent faint. Autumn colour poor. In my experience it has lived up to the 'Issai' name, flowering well as a young plant.

According to Wyman (1949) a plant cultivated at the Arnold Arboretum as 'Issai' is not a true floribunda type, as it climbs by twining in an anticlockwise direction and is probably a hybrid of W. sinensis. However all cultivars which I have seen and to which the name 'Issai' has been applied, either alone or in combination with other words, twine in a clockwise direction and show no evidence of hybridity.

'Domino' is a pleasant plant and could be useful for growing as a bonsai, just in a pot, or as a shrub, particularly where production of blooms early in the life of the plant is a priority. It blooms early in the season.

'Ebicha' Figure 5.16

While I have seen and photographed this cultivar in Japan, I have not grown it or made detailed observations of its characteristics. Nevertheless it is a fine cultivar with comparatively large soft pinkish mauve flowers in racemes up to 60 cm long. Kawarada (1985) describes it as a vigorous plant which flowers well, said to be a seedling of

Figure 5.15   *Wisteria floribunda* 'Domino'

Figure 5.16   *Wisteria floribunda* 'Ebicha'

'Honbeni'. Tsukamoto (1984) says it was introduced at the end of the Meiji Period (1868–1912).
If it is not yet in cultivation outside Japan it certainly should be. 'Ebicha' is the Japanese word
for a purplish red colour.

'Eranthema'

See 'Royal Purple'.

'Flore-Pleno'

See 'Violacea Plena'.

'Fragrantissima'

See *W. sinensis* 'Jako'.

'Fujinami'

Reputedly white and purple. I have not so far
succeeded in tracking it down nor in finding out
what 'Fujinami' means. It has been suggested that
it may be a place name.

'Geisha'   Figure 5.17

According to Bean (1980) this was imported to
Britain from Japan by James Russell. Nowadays

Figure 5.17   *Wisteria floribunda* 'Geisha'

it does not seem to be known in Japan and the only plants I have encountered have come from the W. B. Clarke Nursery Company of San Jose, California, which listed it from 1940 on.

'Geisha' is a vigorous plant with an upright branching habit. The leaves have 11–13 broad leaflets, green when young. The narrow racemes are 27.5–36.0 cm long, densely packed with 129–164 small, pale blue, faintly scented flowers; the long-pointed deciduous floral bracts mauve; pedicels green with a bluish tinge, 1.2–1.5 cm long, occasionally up to 2 cm; calyx bluish; standard 1.6 cm broad, pale blue with a greenish yellow blotch; wings and keel bluish mauve, darker. It usually produces an abundant crop of pods 10.0–24.5 cm long, with 1–7 tan seeds, spotted and streaked with black (figure 5.18). Autumn colour is poor.

This cultivar is very distinctive on account of its growth habit, its unusually narrow, densely packed racemes of blue flowers, and its large seed pods. In number of flowers per raceme it is exceeded only by the similarly coloured 'Lawrence'.

'Hachifusa'

According to Kawarada (1985) this is an old cultivar, good for bonsai, with racemes 15–20 cm long. In his illustration the flowers appear pale mauve. The name translates as 'Eight Bunches' or 'Eight Flowers', for what reason is unclear. It is sometimes given as 'Yatsubusa', which means the same thing. It appears to be very similar to 'Asagi'.

'Hagoromo Nishiki' Figure 5.19

This is a golden-variegated cultivar which Kawarada (1985) says has racemes 20–30 cm long, comes from Ibaraki prefecture, and keeps its spring leaf colour for a long time. It is also known as 'Miho Nishiki'. 'Nishiki' is a kind of silver brocade and 'Hagoromo' is the name of a cloak worn by a Buddhist angel, so 'Hagoromo

Figure 5.18
Wisteria seeds. *Left to right from the top:* 'Murasaki Kapitan', 'Formosa', 'Royal Purple', *Wisteria floribunda* seedling, blue hybrid seedling (figure 6.8), 'Shiro Noda', 'Macrobotrys' (as 'Naga Noda'), 'Macrobotrys', 'Geisha', 'Violacea Plena', 'Kuchibeni', 'Honbeni', *Wisteria floribunda* pinkish seedling, hybrid seedling, *Wisteria floribunda* bluish seedling, and 'Lawrence'

Figure 5.19   *Wisteria floribunda* 'Hagoromo Nishiki'

Nishiki' could be translated as 'Brocade Angel's Cloak'. 'Miho' is the name of a place where such an angel came down to earth.

The variegated cultivars are admired in Japan for their foliage, particularly as it expands in spring when the effect is most pronounced. For this reason they are usually seen as pot plants. It seems unlikely that they will become popular elsewhere except, perhaps, as bonsai.

'Hichirimen'

See 'Asagi', and also 'Hichirimen' and 'Highirimen' in chapter 7.

'Hitoe Kokuryu'

See 'Royal Purple'.

'Honbeni'   Figures 5.20–5.21

This is the cultivar often listed as 'Rosea'. In the past it has been given unwarranted recognition as a botanical variety or form, *rosea* (Rehder, 1949), having been first described in this manner in 1903. In addition to this, as Japanese nurseries have used the name *W. multijuga rosea* for a

pale pink form, presumably 'Kuchibeni', and *W. multijuga rubra* for the darker one, it seems wise for this and other reasons to avoid 'Rosea' and to use 'Honbeni' ('True Red'), the name used by many Japanese nurserymen. Other synonyms are 'Beni Fuji' ('Red Wisteria'), 'Momoiro' ('Peach Colour') and 'Akabana' ('Red Flower').

To add to the confusion Tsukamoto (1984) says that another pink variety was derived from 'Honbeni' around the seventh or eighth year of the Taisho Period, presumably 1918 or 1919, and given the name 'Shinbeni' ('New Red'). Kawarada (1985) says this is the same colour and has racemes of the same size but has glossier petals. He also says that whereas 'Honbeni' is a weak grower, 'Shinbeni' is vigorous. Goodness knows what the truth of all this is but I have never seen 'Shinbeni' listed by anyone. And whether correctly named or not, plants sold by nurseries in Japan and elsewhere as 'Honbeni' seem to be quite vigorous, so it seems justifiable to continue to use this name.

It is sometimes also listed with the names 'Rubrum', 'Honko' (another rendering of 'True Red') and, more recently and irritatingly, as 'Pink Ice'. Plants I have received as 'Honbeni', 'Pink Ice' and 'Rosea' have proved to be identical. Wohlert (1937) also lists a cultivar with the name 'Alabama', saying 'Origin in Alabama and sold to us as Rosea. As its pink colour is slightly tinted with lavender, we have given the variety the above name to distinguish it from the true Rosea.' Bowden (1976) illustrates it in black and white and says it appears to be a fine cultivar. It may perhaps not differ from 'Honbeni', which at any rate is a lavender pink.

'Honbeni' does not seem to have been noticed outside Japan until this century. Bean (1980) says 'Rosea' was in cultivation in 1903, presumably in Britain, but whether this is so or whether the plant originally accorded the epithet *rosea* was the paler 'Kuchibeni' we probably cannot know, as he does not mention the latter. Wyman (1949) is of the opinion that the original plant in the United States was probably that found in a garden owned by a Japanese years ago in California. He states that the entire place was bought by the late Mr Henry S. Huntington of San Marino primarily to preserve this beautiful vine, and that the Arnold Arboretum received scions of this plant in 1917. A plant named *W. floribunda* f. *rosea* by Rehder and Wilson (1916) was photographed in 1914 growing in the grounds of the Yokohama Nursery Company by Ernest Wilson. But, since Rehder and Wilson do not seem to have been aware that two pink forms existed, we cannot be certain which one this was.

'Honbeni' has leaves with 11–15 leaflets, markedly bronze-green when young. Racemes 32.5–40.0 cm, occasionally up to 45.0 cm, with 72–97 flowers; scent faint to medium; floral bracts purplish; pedicels suffused pinkish purple, 1.5–2.0 cm long; calyx pinkish purple, paling towards the tips of the lobes; standard 1.8–2.0 cm broad, lavender pink, darkest towards the sides, with a yellow blotch, pubescent at the top inside and around the claw outside; wings and keel a little darker, reddish purple at their tips. Pods 8.0–23.5 cm long with 1–5 seeds, pinkish tan, heavily spotted black (figure 5.18). Autumn colour good.

Although the pink colour is definitely on the lavender side, this, combined with the yellow blotch, which grades to white above, gives the impression of a soft delicate pink (figure 5.21). For this reason it ranks among the best cultivars, although, unless trained and pruned carefully (see chapter 8), it is not as reliably floriferous as the paler 'Kuchibeni'. Also, like the latter, the colour varies in depth according to the season, the amount of exposure to sunlight and other environmental influences.

'Honey Bee Pink'

A cultivar name about which little is known. It is tempting to suggest that it is merely a fanciful adaptation of 'Honbeni'.

'Honko'

See 'Honbeni'.

'Issai', 'Issai Fuji'

See 'Domino'.

Figure 5.20 *above* & **figure 5.21** *opposite*
Wisteria floribunda 'Honbeni'

'Issai Naga' Figure 5.22

This name means 'Long Issai'. It blooms early in the season and has leaves with 11–13 broad leaflets, pale bronze-green when young. The racemes are 26–35 cm long with 90–101 flowers; floral bracts purple; pedicels 1.5–2.5 cm, pale green tinged mauve at the ends; standard pale violet, 2 cm broad, pubescent at the top of the inner surface, outer glabrous; wings and keel darker; scent faint. Autumn colour clear yellow.

'Issai Naga' seems close to 'Issai Perfect' as described by Grootendorst (1968). Like 'Domino' it blooms well as a young plant. With its longer racemes each with more individual flowers, one might expect it to prove more effective as an ornamental plant.

'Issai Perfect'

Another cultivar sent to Europe by Koichiro Wada. It was described by Grootendorst (1968) as having leaves with 15 leaflets and 25–35 cm racemes of light lilac blue flowers. As mentioned above, it seems very similar to 'Issai Naga', which also has longer racemes than 'Domino'.

'Ivory Tower'

'Ivory Tower' was found growing on the campus of Princeton University, New Jersey, and introduced by the Princeton Nurseries. It has shorter racemes than 'Shiro Noda', is very fragrant and is a precocious bloomer, often blooming as yearling plants in containers. Although it is claimed to be a cultivar of *W. floribunda*, photographs suggest that it is close to if not identical with *W. sinensis* 'Jako'. Until a detailed examination can be made, its true identity must remain in doubt.

'Izuzu'

See 'Domino'.

'Kawariba'

See 'Nishiki'.

'Kokuryu'

See 'Royal Purple' and 'Violacea Plena'.

'Koshigaya'

See 'Macrobotrys'.

'Kuchibeni' Figures 1.4, 5.12, 5.23, 5.25

This cultivar has been given several names including 'Carnea', 'Alborosea', 'Multijuga Rosea' (as opposed to 'Multijuga Rubra'), 'Akebono' (a poetical expression for 'dawn' or 'daybreak'), 'Lipstick' and 'Peaches and Cream'. The last-mentioned is far too depressing to countenance, as is 'Lipstick', a translation of 'Kuchibeni', an old word which has come to be used for lipstick after its introduction to Japan. A literal translation would perhaps be 'Red Mouth', but anyone looking at the characters would see in them a far more romantic meaning. 'Beni' was originally a red paste of plant origin used for reddening the lips for special occasions. For this reason, and because transliterations rather than translations are recommended by the Code, it seems only reasonable to stay with this charming old Japanese name. 'Akebono', while equally pleasing, is sometimes used for the pink form of *W. brachybotrys* and is therefore likely to lead to confusion.

The leaves have 9–15 leaflets, pale green when young. It is among the earliest to bloom, the racemes being 36–45 cm long with 76–86 flowers; scent moderate; floral bracts tinged with purple; pedicels 1.5–2.5 cm, pale green, sometimes tinged purple towards their ends; calyx pale greyish purple; standard pale mauve-pink, 1.8–2.0 cm broad, conspicuously pubescent at the top inside and around the claw outside, sometimes with a few hairs extending up the mid-line; wings and keel a similar colour but purple at their tips. The pods are 9.0–21.5 cm long with 1–5 seeds, tan finely spotted with black (figure 5.18). The autumn colour is a good clear yellow (figure 5.25).

Figure 5.22
Wisteria floribunda 'Issai Naga'

Figure 5.23
Wisteria floribunda 'Kuchibeni'

Figure 5.24
Wisteria floribunda 'Lawrence'

'Kuchibeni' is very beautiful when opening but the colour fades rapidly in sunlight. Hence it is best grown as a standard or on a pergola, so that the racemes are shaded and can be viewed from beneath. All the same this cultivar can be relied upon to flower abundantly year after year, is nicely scented, has handsome foliage and good autumn colour, all features which make it one of the best for general cultivation.

It seems that there are slightly different forms in cultivation, some a little richer in colour, with the calyx a pronounced bluish grey and some pigmentation on the rachis. Even so the differences in colour which can be discerned on a single plant between shaded racemes and those in full light make these variations difficult to define.

Kawarada (1985) says that the 'Kuchibeni' type can be found growing wild in the San-in area and on Shikoku and Kyushu, hence one would expect some variation.

'Kyushaku'

See 'Macrobotrys'.

'Lavender Lace'

See chapter 6.

'Lawrence'　　　　　　　Figure 5.24, 9.1

According to Bowden (1976) this was discovered in May 1970 growing on a cottage in Lawrence Street, Brentford, Ottawa, Canada, and he suggests that the plant from which it was propagated may have come from England. Whatever its origin it is the best pale blue cultivar I have seen.

'Lawrence' produces leaves with 11–17 leaflets, green when young. The racemes are 36.5–49.0 cm long, densely packed with 145–170 sweetly scented flowers; floral bracts pale green suffused violet; pedicels 1.5–2.5 cm, pale green tinged violet towards the calyx; calyx bluish; standard pale blue-violet, 1.7–2.0 cm broad, with a greenish yellow blotch; wings and keel darker. Large pods produced abundantly with 1–5 seeds, light tan with moderate black spotting and streaking (figure 5.18). The autumn colour is a good clear yellow.

With its long racemes, pale blue flowers, floriferousness and good autumn colour, 'Lawrence' is highly recommended. No other cultivar I have seen produces as many flowers per raceme.

'Lipstick'

See 'Kuchibeni'.

'Longissima'

See 'Macrobotrys'.

'Longissima Alba'

See 'Shiro Noda'.

'Longissima Plena'

See 'Violacea Plena'.

'Longissima Rosea Plena'

See 'Violacea Plena'.

'Macrobotrys'   Figs 2.1, 5.3–5.5, 5.10, 5.26–5.28

From descriptions and illustrations it is clear that an exceptionally long-racemed form or forms of *W. floribunda* have been known in Japan for at least 400 years. The length of the racemes results not so much from the number of flowers as their spacing, ranging from an average of about 2 mm in 'Geisha' to 6 or 7 mm in 'Macrobotrys'. This phenomenon is thus presumably the result of a mutation affecting the rachis.

Be all that as it may, 'Macrobotrys' is one of the world's great garden plants, fully deserving the rave reviews of it given by Kaempfer (1712, 1736), Siebold (1835–41), Fortune (1863) and Du Cane (1908). To sit or stand beneath a pergola covered by a plant in full bloom, gazing at the mauve curtain of flowers, inhaling the scent and listening to the bees, is one of the most intoxicating of horticultural experiences.

Figure 5.26 *Wisteria floribunda* 'Macrobotrys', Nooroo, Mount Wilson, NSW, in autumn

Figure 5.25 *previous pages* *Wisteria floribunda* 'Kuchibeni' in autumn

Figure 5.27   *Wisteria floribunda* 'Macrobotrys'

Figure 5.28 *Wisteria floribunda* 'Macrobotrys', Nooroo, Mount Wilson, NSW, in spring

Based on observations made in recent years on plants in my family's garden and elsewhere, this cultivar is described as follows: leaves with 11–17 leaflets, usually 15, pale bronze when young. Racemes 47–100 cm long, sometimes longer, with 79–128 moderately scented flowers; floral bracts purplish; pedicels 1.5–1.9 cm, green, purplish towards the calyx; calyx purple; standard 1.8–2.0 cm broad, pale violet with a yellow blotch, pubescent at the top inside, outside around the claw and sparsely up the mid-line; wings and keel darker. Pods 11.0–20.5 cm with 1–6 seeds, tan, sparsely and finely spotted black (figure 5.18). Autumn colour good.

But what name should we give this wonderful plant? I have received it under the names 'Multijuga', 'Murasaki Naga', 'Purple Patches', 'Naga Noda', 'Longissima' and 'Kyushaku'. And is there more than one variant of this type? These are questions which are hard to answer. By making comparisons of leaflet number, flowering time, flower spacing and so on I can detect no differences between the plants I have obtained bearing the above names. Nor do they seem any different from the famous wisteria at Ushijima and others I have been able to examine in Japan.

Other names result from introductions being named after the locality of the vine from which the propagation was made, for example 'Penn Valley Long Cluster', 'Koshigaya' and 'Ushijima'. Propagations from the Ushijima wisteria are known generally as 'Kyushaku'. A shaku is a Japanese measure of length, approximately 25 cm (10 inches), and 'Kyushaku' means 'Nine Shaku'. Others have been similarly named on account of the length of their racemes, for example 'Rokushaku' ('Six Shaku'), 'Sanshaku' ('Three Shaku'), which is propagated from Kuroki-no-fuji, Fukuoka prefecture, or even just 'Naga Fuji' ('Long Wisteria'). The Ushijima wisteria was called 'Seven Foot Wisteria' by Dorsett (1935) and

the Koshigaya wisteria 'Five Foot Wisteria'. Wohlert (1937) gives 'Five Foot Wisteria' as an alternative name for 'Naga Noda'. 'Naga Noda' is sometimes written as 'Noda Naga' and, according to Kawarada (1985), the name applies to propagations from the Yuya-no-naga-fuji of Shizuoka prefecture. In addition Uehara (1961) gives 'Naga-ho-no-fuji' ('Long-racemed Wisteria') as a synonym of 'Macrobotrys'.

But as anyone who has grown 'Macrobotrys' will know, the length of the racemes varies from season to season, according to the locality and with the age and vigour of the plant. For instance, as already mentioned, in 1914 Wilson (1916) measured a raceme 1.64 m long on the Ushijima wisteria near Kasukabe (figure 5.4). When P. H. Dorsett (1935) visited it in May 1929 he measured racemes up to 1.2 m (figure 5.10), and when I visited it recently the longest racemes were only about 90 cm. The longest raceme measured on 'Macrobotrys' in my family's garden was 1.2 m forty years ago, but nowadays only on the rarest occasions does a raceme exceed a metre.

As described earlier it seems that it was in the form of this cultivar that W. floribunda was first introduced to Europe, following which it was named W. multijuga by Louis van Houtte in 1873. Bean (1980) gives this cultivar the name 'Multijuga', but this can lead to confusion as introductions of other cultivars have been included under this name, for example W. multijuga alba, W. multijuga rosea and so on. Hence it seems best to stay with 'Macrobotrys', which means 'large bunch', though it is tempting to give 'Kyushaku' precedence as the cultivar name.

At present it must remain uncertain as to whether all the long-racemed wisterias are the same. Kawarada (1985) does not think so and says, for instance, that 'Rokushaku', which comes from a plant at Kumano, is often confused with 'Kyushaku' but is paler. Meanwhile it seems sensible to continue to use the name 'Macrobotrys' for the form now so widely grown outside Japan.

There is an old plant growing at the Ellerslie Racecourse, Auckland, New Zealand, which exhibits definite differences. The flowers (figure 5.29) are a pinker mauve than 'Macrobotrys' in racemes up to 1.06 m long with up to 132 flowers, that is, averaging 8 mm apart. The hairs on the outer surface of the standard do not extend up the midline as in 'Macrobotrys', and the young leaves are yellow-green rather than bronze-green. Also the midribs of the leaves are suffused with purple, which has not been seen in 'Macrobotrys'. Whether this is a local seedling or a form imported from Japan is not known, but I understand it will be named and distributed.

'Miho Nishiki'

See 'Hagoromo Nishiki'.

'Momoiro'

See 'Honbeni'.

'Mon Nishiki'

See 'Nishiki'.

'Multijuga'

See 'Macrobotrys'.

'Multijuga Alba'

See 'Shiro Noda'.

'Multijuga Flore-Pleno'

See 'Violacea Plena'.

'Multijuga Fragrans'

It is not known to what this name refers but it is suggested that, since a plant from Japan labelled *W. floribunda* 'Fragrantissima' turned out to be *W. sinensis* 'Jako', this might be the same.

'Multijuga Praecox'

See 'Domino'.

Figure 5.29 *Wisteria floribunda*, very long racemed form, Auckland, New Zealand

'Multijuga Rosea'

See 'Honbeni' and 'Kuchibeni'.

'Multijuga Rubra'

See 'Honbeni'.

'Murasaki Fuji', 'Murasaki Noda'

These names merely mean purple-flowered *W. floribunda* and refer to relatively short-racemed forms offered from time to time by nurseries.

'Murasaki Naga', 'Murasaki Naga Fuji'

See 'Macrobotrys'.

'Naga Fuji', 'Naga-ho-no-fuji'

See 'Macrobotrys'.

'Naga Noda'

See 'Macrobotrys'.

Figure 5.30   *Wisteria floribunda* 'Nagasaki Issai'

Figure 5.31   *Wisteria floribunda* 'Nishiki'

'Nagasaki Issai'   Figure 5.30

This short-racemed form is notable for having the wings and keel very much darker than the standard. Kawarada (1985) says grafted plants bloom in three to four years and that it is grown widely in the Kansai area.

The leaves have 11–13 broadly ovate leaflets, pale bronze-green when young. The racemes are 17.5–31.0 cm long, with 37–58 faintly scented flowers; floral bracts dark purplish; pedicels 2.0–2.8 cm, green suffused mauve; calyx purple, green at the lobes; standard 1.8 cm broad, blue-violet with a yellow blotch, pubescent at the top inside and around the claw outside; wings violet, darkest at the tips; keel violet, very dark at the tip. Autumn colour good.

Worth growing for the comparatively rich colour of the flowers. Plants I have imported with this name have paler flowers and look very similar to 'Domino'.

'Namban Fuji'

See 'Violacea Plena'.

'Nana Richins Purple'

This is not a dwarf cultivar but was imported from Japan with this name. When comparisons can be made it will be possible to decide whether or not it is a distinct form.

'Nioi Fuji'

Tsukamoto (1984) lists this name for a cultivar with scented flowers in racemes only 20 cm long. Likewise Makino et al. (1955) give 'Nioi Fuji' as a cultivar of *W. floribunda*. 'Nioi' means 'fragrant' and is also used for the cultivar of *W. sinensis* more commonly known as 'Jako'.

'Nishiki'   Figure 5.31

Also known as 'Variegata', 'Albomaculata', 'Kawariba' ('Different Leaf') and 'Mon Nishiki'

('Crested Brocade'). According to Rehder (1949) it was first described in the West in 1887 as *W. multijuga* var. *variegata* in Nicholson's *Illustrated Dictionary of Gardening*, so presumably it had been introduced to Britain prior to this. It is apparently an old Japanese cultivar, usually grown in pots for the appearance of its leaves which are very ornamental when young. As with many variegated plants it regularly produces fully green shoots. Hence these must be cut out as they appear if the variegation is not to be lost. I have not seen the flowers but Kawarada (1985) says that the racemes are about 15 cm long with flowers the colour of the wild type.

The foliage is very characteristic, the leaves being composed of 11–17 narrow leaflets, wavy at the margins, cream spotted green when young, the green areas becoming more prominent as the leaves mature. Autumn colour poor.

It is not known whether the plant listed as 'Shin Nishiki' ('New Nishiki') is the same or a different variegated cultivar.

'Noda Issai'

See 'Royal Purple'.

'Noda Naga'

Merely another way of writing 'Naga Noda'. See 'Multijuga'.

'Peaches and Cream'

See 'Kuchibeni'.

'Penn Valley Long Cluster'

See 'Macrobotrys'.

'Pink Ice'

See 'Honbeni'.

'Pleniflora'

See 'Violacea Plena'.

'Praecox'

See 'Domino'.

'Praecox Odorata Alba'

See *W. sinensis* 'Jako'.

'Praecox White'

See *W. sinensis* 'Jako'.

'Prematura'

See 'Domino'.

'Prematura Alba'

See *W. brachybotrys* 'Shiro Kapitan'.

'Purple Patches'

See 'Macrobotrys'.

'Rokushaku'

See 'Macrobotrys'.

'Rosea'

See 'Honbeni'.

'Royal Purple'   Figure 5.32

This excellent, strongly coloured cultivar is something of a mystery. The first reference to it which I have seen is in the catalogue of A. E. Wohlert (1937) where it is described as 'Multijuga form, deep violet color, out of the ordinary and very striking. Clusters 15–18 inches [38–46 cm] long.' Whether it came from Japan and was renamed or arose in the United States is unclear, as it does not seem to have been listed by Japanese nurseries under any name until relatively recently. The chief source of its distribution in the West seems to have been the W. B. Clarke Nursery Company of San Jose, California.

In Japan it is now known under the names 'Noda Issai' ('Early-maturing *W. floribunda*'), 'Kokuryu' ('Black Dragon'), and 'Hitoe Kokuryu'

Figure 5.32 *Wisteria floribunda* 'Royal Purple'

('Single Black Dragon'). In spite of their appeal, the last two names are confusing as the double form of *W. floribunda* is called 'Yae Kokuryu' ('Double Black Dragon') in Japan. The name 'Noda Issai' alludes to its blooming as a relatively young plant, but in view of the imprecision associated with the words 'Noda' and 'Issai', 'Royal Purple' seems the only name unlikely to cause confusion.

As a gamble I imported from Japan plants listed as *W. brachybotrys* 'Eranthema'. It is hard to imagine where such a name could have come from, but when the plants bloomed they proved to be identical with 'Royal Purple, so that, yet again, was that.

'Royal Purple' produces leaves with 11–15 narrow leaflets, pale bronze-green when young.

The racemes are 27–40 cm long, occasionally up to 52 cm, with 91–109 sweetly scented flowers; floral bracts pale mauve with a green edge; pedicels purplish, 1.8–3.0 cm long; calyx purple, paler at the lobes; standard violet, 2.0–2.1 cm broad, pubescent at the top inside and around the claw outside, the blotch appearing very distinct owing to the depth of the colour surrounding it; wings and keel a little darker. Pods produced abundantly, 9.5–25.5 cm long with 1–8 seeds, tan, heavily spotted and streaked black (figure 5.18). Autumn colour good.

Flowering early in life and in the season, reliable and floriferous, with a neat growth habit and good autumn colour, this cultivar is highly recommended. It is the darkest of all the single-flowered named cultivars I have seen, though plants of 'Nagasaki Issai' seen in Japan produced a similar effect, but with much shorter racemes.

'Royal Robe'

Known to me as a name only.

'Rubrum'

See 'Honbeni'.

'Russelliana'

This frequently mentioned cultivar seems difficult to track down. Any plants with this name that I have encountered have turned out to be something else. As far as I know it is not at present listed by any nursery.

It was originally described (*Gardening World* 1904) as having a soft purple standard deepening in colour with age on both faces and with a creamy white eye-like blotch on the inner face, the colour of the flowers being very much darker than in *W. multijuga* (that is, 'Macrobotrys'). The coloured illustration accompanying the description shows a plant with bronze young leaves with 11 leaflets and a raceme of 51 flowers, but it is reported that on strong growing shoots the ra-cemes varied in length from 46 to 84 cm. This description was based on a plant growing in a pot in the nursery of Mr John Russell at Rich-mond, Surrey, on 22 June 1903.

It is tempting to suggest that this and 'Royal Purple' may be identical, but 'Russelliana', at least under the conditions prevailing at the time of its original description, was in bloom very late in the season. There is an unnamed plant in the gar-den at Filoli, Woodside, California, which fits the description of 'Russelliana'. I saw it there still in bloom on 9 May 1990, long after all other wis-terias in the garden were over.

Whether the true 'Russelliana' is still in culti-vation and whether it differs from 'Royal Purple' remains to be seen.

'Sairo Nira'

See 'Shiro Noda'.

'Sanshaku'

See 'Macrobotrys'.

'Sekine's Blue'

Like 'Russelliana', this cultivar is mentioned re-peatedly in the literature but appears no longer to be listed by nurserymen, although perhaps it survives in gardens.

Wyman (1949, 1961) reported its cultivation at the Arnold Arboretum and recorded it as hav-ing 'Clusters seven inches [17.8 cm]; little fragrance; 17 leaflets; standard whitish, wings and keel sea lavender violet 637/2.' If this descrip-tion is a reliable guide, it may be that its disap-pearance is no great loss.

'Shibori'

See 'Asagi'.

'Shinbeni'

See 'Honbeni'.

'Shinku'

This name means 'crimson' but to what it refers I do not know. Perhaps it may be the same as 'Satsuma Sakuko Fuji' described in chapter 7.

'Shin Nishiki'

See 'Nishiki'.

'Shioori'

A mysterious name which seems not to be a proper Japanese word. It might be a misspelling of 'Shiro' and thus perhaps the same as 'Shiro Noda'. It is also possibly a misspelling of 'Shibori' (see 'Asagi').

'Shirobana'

See 'Shiro Noda'.

'Shiro Naga'

See 'Shiro Noda'.

'Shiro Noda'   **Figures 5.1, 5.7, 5.33–5.35, 9.2**

One of the most beautiful of all wisterias, this long-racemed, late-flowering cultivar should be in every collection. It has undoubtedly been grown in Japan for a long time. Whether the white wisteria planted by Ashikaga Yoshimasa in 1461 (Kawarada 1985) was this cultivar we cannot know. However, on the walls of the room over-looking the Tiger Glen Garden at Nishi Honganji in Kyoto mentioned earlier, a long-racemed white wisteria is depicted, the painting possibly dating from the late sixteenth century. And in the National Museum in Tokyo there is a wonderful pair of eighteenth century six-fold screens deco-rated by Kano Hakuen with a single blossoming plant growing over a bamboo frame. No doubt a search might reveal that it has frequently been painted over the centuries.

Although Kawarada (1985) says that white forms with racemes 20–30 cm long occur wild in the San-in area and I saw a similar white form on a roadside bank near Wondok in South Korea, it has been my experience, and that of Japanese horticulturalists to whom I have spoken, that there is only one white form in general cultivation in Japan, albeit under a variety of names. Those I have noticed include 'Shiro Noda' ('White *W. floribunda*'), 'Shiro Naga' ('Long White'), 'Shiro Bana' ('White Flower'), 'Showa Shiro' ('White of the Showa Era'), 'Wase Shiro Naga' ('Early-maturing Long White'), 'Alba', 'Multijuga Alba', 'Longissima Alba', and 'Snow Showers'. According to Tsukamoto (1984) it was called 'Wase Shiro Naga' in the Taisho Period (1912–26) but that this was changed to 'Showa Shiro' during the Showa Period (1926–89), Emperor Hirohito's reign. It may be that 'Silver Lace', mentioned by Bowden (1976), belongs here too. A strange name appearing in some lists is 'Sairo Nira', which could perhaps be a misspelling of 'Shiro Noda' or 'Shiro Naga'. According to Rehder (1949), it was first described in Europe in 1890 by C. de Vos as *Glycine multijuga alba* and in the following year described and figured as *W. multijuga alba* by Carrière, so presumably it had been introduced some time shortly before.

Of all the names mentioned above, I have chosen to recommend 'Shiro Noda', which is widely used in Japan. I have rejected 'Alba' as it has been used earlier for a white cultivar of *W. sinensis*.

This plant has leaves with 11–15 leaflets, pale green when young. The racemes 36.0–47.5 cm long, occasionally more, densely packed with 129–153 flowers; scent faint; floral bracts pale green; pedicels pale green, to 2 cm, often not twisting fully through 180 degrees so that some flowers are not held fully upright; calyx bluish grey, white towards the teeth, bottom tooth long; standard 1.5–1.8 cm broad, edges becoming reflexed so that it often appears narrower, pubescent at the top inside, glabrous outside except for

Figure 5.33 *Wisteria floribunda* 'Shiro Noda'

a few hairs on the claw, pure white except for the yellow blotch; wings pure white; keel white, violet at the tip. Pods long, 11–31 cm, with 2–8 seeds; seeds pale tan with no darker streaking or spotting (figure 5.18). Autumn colour poor.

The above description holds for all plants I have grown or seen under whatever name. The cultivar is easily recognised by its densely packed racemes of white flowers, the pale green of its young leaves, the length of its pods, the colour of its seeds and the lateness of its blooming and

Figure 5.34   *Wisteria floribunda* 'Shiro Noda'

Figure 5.35   *Wisteria floribunda* 'Shiro Noda' on the Japanese bridge at Giverny.

leafing. It no doubt may produce longer racemes under the most favourable conditions, but it must be remembered that the measurements I have made are from the attachment of the first flower and do not include the leafy peduncle. In number of flowers per raceme it is exceeded only by 'Geisha' and 'Lawrence'.

While not as impressive as many, the plant of this cultivar known best in the West is probably that growing on the Japanese bridge in Monet's garden at Giverny (figure 5.35). It is also used in France with great effect on a series of arches in the garden at Apremont. To my mind it is the most beautiful of the white wisterias, arousing the admiration of all who see it.

'Showa Shiro'

See 'Shiro Noda'.

'Silver Lace'

See 'Shiro Noda'.

'Snow Showers'

See 'Shiro Noda'.

'Ushijima'

See 'Macrobotrys'.

'Variegata'

See 'Nishiki'.

'Violacea Plena'   Figures 5.36–5.37

As far as I have been able to ascertain, this is the only double-flowered wisteria in existence. Not only this, but it produces the darkest coloured flowers, though the colour may vary a great deal

Figure 5.36   *Wisteria floribunda* 'Violacea Plena' in autumn

Figure 5.37   *Wisteria floribunda* 'Violacea Plena'

according to conditions, a state of affairs which has led to some disagreement among growers as to whether there are one or more double cultivars in existence.

In the past this plant has been given botanical status as a variety or form with the name *violaceo-plena, flore-pleno* or *pleniflora* (Rehder 1949). As is generally the case in *Wisteria* there is no justification for this and it should be regarded as a cultivar. The W. B. Clarke Nursery at one time or another also listed the Latin names 'Longissima Plena' and 'Longissima Rosea Plena', but these were not repeated, presumably because the plants proved to be 'Violacea Plena' or something else.

Cultivar names which have been used for this plant are 'Yae Fuji' ('Double Wisteria'), 'Yae Kokuryu' ('Double Black Dragon'), 'Kokuryu' ('Black Dragon'), 'Botan Fuji' ('Peony Wisteria'), 'Multijuga Flore-Pleno' and 'Violacea Plena'. Another Japanese name for this cultivar is 'Namban Fuji'. 'Namban' means 'Southern Barbarian', a name given to Europeans in the early days of contact. The kindest interpretation I can put on this is that the word is used here in the sense of 'rare' or 'exotic'.

Much as I would like to give my blessing to one of the Japanese names, these are either obscure or include the word 'Kokuryu', which, along with its English translation 'Black Dragon', has led to confusion. Thus we are left with the old Latin name 'Violacea Plena'.

'Violacea Plena', according to Mr Kawarada (personal communication), originally came from the Kasuga Shrine at Nara. Wyman (1949) says it first flowered in North America in the garden of Francis Parkman of Jamaica Plain, Massachusetts, before 1875, and Bean (1980) says it was introduced to the United States from Japan in the 1860s and thence to Britain about 1870. It was first named *W. sinensis flore pleno* by Carrière

(1878), which has resulted in the confusion discussed in the previous chapter under *W. sinensis* 'Plena'.

The doubling of the flowers results, as in most species, from an increase in the number of petals, largely as a consequence of the transformation of the stamens into petals or petal-like structures. Boehmer's (1903) statement that each single blossom looks like a double violet is particularly apt.

The leaves have 9–13 leaflets, usually 13, pale bronze when young, becoming broad and slightly bullate (convex between the veins). The racemes are 33.5–36.5 cm long with 75–86 flowers; scent faint; floral bracts pale green tinged mauve; pedicels 1.5–3.5 cm long, green suffused purple; calyx purple, paler towards the lobes; each flower consisting of about 20 petal-like elements, the inner 15 being dark violet at their tips, which gives the flowers, which may be 2.0–3.5 cm in diameter, considerable richness of colour. In spite of the usual absence of stamens, occasional pods develop containing 2–6 large medium-brown seeds, finely streaked, spotted and blotched black (figure 5.18). The autumn colour is clear butter-yellow, the best of all the cultivars (figure 5.36).

It is difficult to get 'Violacea Plena' to flower young and it is often stated that it is not floriferous. However if it is grown in full sun and carefully pruned, it can be as floriferous as any cultivar. And in autumn the warm yellow of the bold foliage is particularly pleasing.

'Wase Shiro Naga'

See 'Shiro Noda'.

'White with Blue Eye'

This is listed by the Louisiana Nursery and is described as having showy racemes of fragrant white flowers with blue centres. Presumably the standard is white and the wings and keel blue or blue-violet. The description is very like that given for 'Sekine's Blue' by Wyman (1949).

It has not yet flowered for me but, although it is not listed under any species name by the Louisiana Nursery, in its vegetative characters it appears to be a form of *W. floribunda*.

'Yae Fuji'

See 'Violacea Plena'.

'Yae Kokuryu'

See 'Violacea Plena'.

'Yatsubusa'

See 'Hachifusa'.

OTHER CULTIVARS

There exist numerous other attractive forms which must be either cultivars the names of which have been lost or unnamed seedlings. For instance, according to Bean (1980), James Comber raised many seedlings at Nymans in Sussex, the best of which were the equal of the named sorts, and E. A. Bowles had a home-raised seedling in his garden at Myddleton House.

In the Japanese garden at the Brooklyn Botanic Garden there are pale and dark forms unlike anything I have seen elsewhere, and in other parts of the garden there are some charming pale blues. Likewise at the Arnold Arboretum there is an excellent pale blue form with long racemes growing on a boundary fence. And growing in the garden of an old house at Balmain, Sydney, there is a plant with flowers of an unusually rich purple (figure 5.38).

From among seedlings it is possible to select forms with racemes 20–40 cm long with 80–100 flowers ranging from bluish violet to reddish violet, which are excellent garden plants. Undoubtedly many such types occur in gardens as a result of the rootstock of grafted plants having outgrown

the scion. Among plants of mine where this has happened some have been well worth keeping, notably a floriferous pinkish mauve with racemes 32–57 cm long with 98–108 flowers.

Another plant I might mention here came from Japan as *W. brachybotrys* 'Rosea'. It is however a form of *W. floribunda*, the leaves of which have 13–15 broad, oblong leaflets, pale bronze-green when young. The racemes are 31.5–36.5 cm long with 101–110 strongly scented flowers; floral bracts pale green, relatively large; pedicels green, 1.5–1.8 cm; calyx whitish, marked with bluish violet, the lobes white; standard white with a yellow blotch, 2.0–2.5 cm in diameter, broader than tall; wings white, tinged pale violet at the tips;

Figure 5.38 *Wisteria floribunda*, dark form, Balmain, NSW

Figure 5.39 *Wisteria floribunda* form received as *Wisteria brachybotrys* 'Rosea'

keel white with a deep violet tip (figure 5.39). Autumn colour clear yellow, very good.

This variant is very distinctive with its densely packed racemes and standard which is broader than tall. It should prove worth propagating.

W. *brachybotrys* Sieb. & Zucc.

SILKY WISTERIA, YAMA FUJI

If ever there was a plant deserving to be better known it is this wisteria. With its broad racemes of scented, heavy-textured flowers appearing early in the season, it is surprising that it is not as common as *W. sinensis*, particularly since there are

white, pink and mauve cultivars. Perhaps confusion concerning its true identity is to blame. Hence it is hoped that what follows will help sort things out.

The Royal Horticultural Society was encouraged to stage its first Chelsea Flower Show in 1913 by the success of the Royal International Horticultural Exhibition held in the grounds of the Chelsea Hospital in 1912. This had been organised by Harry James Veitch, the well-known horticulturalist and nurseryman, who was subsequently knighted for his efforts. In the Japanese section of this exhibition were shown some white wisterias grown as shrubs and labelled 'W. *brachybotrys*'. This was apparently the first time this wisteria had been seen in Britain, and the following year it was imported from Yokohama for Kew, though it had already been listed by the Yokohama Nursery Company for some years.

It had earlier been noticed in Japanese gardens by Florence Du Cane (1908), who let her pen run away with the following: 'The last petals of the cherry blossoms have only just fallen, and Nature hastens to provide a new treasure for the flower kingdom, as the first blooms of the wistaria *Fuji no hana* will be opening at the base of the quickly growing racemes. Not the far-famed *Wistaria multijuga*, whose immense long sprays of delicate mauve flowers are so associated throughout the world with the name of Japan, but the early-flowering wistaria, *Brachybotris*, with its tufts of white blossoms completely covering the closely pruned branches before any trace of a leaf appears. It would seem as if this modest white wistaria had been allowed to bloom so early, for fear she should be overlooked and not appreciated when her showy successor flings her purple mantle over the land.'

This white wisteria was described as a new species, *W. venusta*, by Rehder and Wilson (1916), working at the Arnold Arboretum. Wilson had collected it from several gardens in Japan in 1914 and had photographed an old plant growing on a pergola at Nara (figure 5.40). In 1919 it was illustrated in *Curtis's Botanical Magazine* (Prain 1919). In the text accompanying this illustration it was stated that the colour of the flowers would appear to vary, as a specimen collected wild on the hills near Nagasaki by Mr R. Oldham in 1863, which undoubtedly belongs to this species, was noted by him as having bluish violet flowers.

It was also pointed out that the species is easily distinguished by, among other things, its downy leaves, its short, broad racemes, its stout spreading velvety pedicels, and its large flowers (figures 5.41, 5.45) and that on this basis it was extraordinary that its right to be recognised as a separate species had remained so long unrecognised.

As it happens, this was not the case. In Japan it had long been known as 'Yama Fuji' ('Mountain Wisteria'), and the white form as 'Shira Fuji' ('White Wisteria'), these forms being distinguished from *W. floribunda*, which is known simply as 'Fuji' or 'Noda Fuji'.

While the white form apparently was not noticed by Kaempfer, Thunberg or Siebold, according to Miyazawa (1940) the *Hanafu* (*Flower Calendar*) of the late seventeenth century mentions the cultivation of 'Yama Fuji'. In addition both white and blue large-flowered, short-racemed wisterias are depicted on scrolls and screens of the seventeenth, eighteenth and nineteenth centuries. It is highly unlikely that these are forms of *W. floribunda* as they are often depicted with it, the individual flowers being shown as larger and in racemes of only about 12–25.

As already mentioned in relation to *W. floribunda*, Western knowledge of Japanese wisterias begins with Engelbert Kaempfer, who listed 'Jamma Fuji' in his *Amoenitatum Exoticarum* (1712) and described its leaves as being 'flocculisque minoribus' (covered with down). So considering his restricted movements it must have been sufficiently common for him to have noticed it. In the posthumously published version of his manuscripts (1736) he describes it as growing wild, having leaves and flowers smaller than the ordinary 'fudsi' and racemes which are not pendant. I assume that by 'smaller leaves' he meant 'with fewer leaflets' and by 'smaller flowers', 'shorter racemes'.

It came to notice again 130 years later when it was collected by Siebold. He noticed it here and there in gardens but found it wild only once not far from Nagasaki, near the village of Koseido on the edge of the sea, and described its blue-indigo flowers as making a fine effect with the soft russet-green leaves (Siebold & Zuccarini 1835–41).

On his return a description of it was published in volume 1 of Siebold's and Zuccarini's *Flora Japonica* (1835–41). Here it was given the specific epithet *brachybotrys* (short-clustered) and again it was noted that its Japanese name was 'Jamma Fudsi'. Since this was the first occasion on which it had been described and given a botanical name, one must be forgiven for assuming that it should be called *W. brachybotrys* Sieb. & Zucc., the name which Japanese botanists are content to use.

Why then did Rehder and Wilson ignore all this when they named the white form *W. venusta*? It seems to be the result of Wilson's announcing (1916) that Siebold's and Zuccarini's *W. brachybotrys* 'is nothing but a condition of *W. floribunda*, and I have collected from wild plants in the spring season specimens in which the inflorescence measures from 10–35 cm. The very short racemes (10 cm) are rare on plants in the spring-time, but they may commonly be seen in the late summer, when some plants bear a sparse second crop of flowers.' He also says that 'the vernacular name given by Siebold and Zuccarini should have

Figure 5.40   *Wisteria brachybotrys* 'Shiro Kapitan' at Nara, 25 April 1914 (E. H. Wilson)

Figure 5.41   *Wisteria brachybotrys* 'Shiro Kapitan'

established its identity long ago, for vernacular names are remarkably constant in Japan.'

A surprising opinion when it is clear that 'Fuji' and 'Yama Fuji' appear to have been consistently applied to the two different species at least since Kaempfer's time. One wonders whether he actually looked at Siebold's and Zuccarini's illustration, which shows a silky-hairy plant with short stout racemes of 10–14 flowers, whereas their illustration of *W. floribunda* (as *W. chinensis*) shows a less hairy plant with a long slender raceme of about 50 smaller flowers. Also the illustrations correctly show the apex of the keel of *W. brachybotrys* as broadly rounded and that of *W. floribunda* as narrowly so.

Unfortunately Wilson's considering *W. brachybotrys* to be a synonym of *W. floribunda* seems to have been generally accepted outside Japan, with the result that the name *W. venusta* has been used ever since for the plant under consideration. However, if my interpretation of all this is correct, this name should be abandoned. It was only based on a cultivar in the first place, and I am sure everyone would soon get used to the change. This would also get rid of other problems caused by Wilson's conclusion as, when translations or abstracts are made of Japanese writings about *W. brachybotrys*, it has been generally assumed that it is to *W. floribunda* that they properly apply, when this is not the case. When the Japanese refer to a plant as *W. brachybotrys* they do *not* mean *W. floribunda*.

In spite of the excitement caused by the appearance of the white form in London in 1912, it seems that a violet form had arrived in Europe much earlier. According to Spae (1847) it was introduced by Siebold from Japan in 1830 to the botanic garden at Ghent and Spae's illustration shows a raceme of 22 flowers and leaves with 9–13 leaflets. This information was repeated by Planchon (1853), again with an illustration, this time showing a raceme of 30 flowers and leaves with nine leaflets.

Siebold's plant does not appear to have persisted in cultivation in Europe, perhaps because in the garden it seemed merely a shorter racemed version of *W. sinensis*. A violet form has only recently been reintroduced to Europe.

In the United States a violet form was introduced by W. B. Clarke of California in whose catalogues it is listed from 1939 on as *W. venusta* 'Violacea', having earlier been given the status of a botanical form, *violacea*, by Rehder (1926). I imported it in 1963 from the J. Clarke Nursery Company, the successor to W. B. Clarke, and subsequently from sources in Japan

It seems a shame to have subjected the reader to this preamble, but otherwise it would be impossible to describe and correctly name this beautiful species and its cultivars. Apart from its white form, *W. brachybotrys* is generally unknown outside Japan. I feel certain that this situation will change as the qualities of the violet, pink and mauve-pink cultivars become recognised.

In Japan *W. brachybotrys,* like *W. floribunda*, has uses other than its being grown for ornament. According to George Usher (1974), the bark fibres are used for making cloth. And Kaneko et al. (1988) record that the galls developing on this plant as a result of infection by the bacterium *Erwinia millettiae* (*E. herbicola* pv. *millettiae*) are used in Japanese folk medicine as an anti-inflammatory agent. This has led to the analysis of extracts from these galls for the presence of active compounds. Konoshima et al. (1988, 1989, 1991) report the use of these galls for the treatment of gastric cancer and have isolated compounds capable of inhibiting skin tumour promotion by the Epstein-Barr virus. A similar compound has been isolated from wisteria seeds (Norimura et al. 1990). It may prove that this research will lead to the development of some useful drugs.

DESCRIPTION

Unfortunately I have not seen the plant growing wild but I have raised plants from seeds collected by Yuri Kurashige in October 1992 near the Ishimi River, Nichinan, Tottori, Honshu. At the time of writing they have not yet flowered but have enabled me to observe characteristics of the foliage and the direction of twining. Also I have examined at Kew a flowering specimen collected at Mount Hyonosen, about 100 km further east, in May 1968. On the basis of these observations I offer the following description of the wild plant.

Vigorous deciduous climber, twining anti-clockwise. Leaves with 9–11 leaflets, shortly pubescent above and below, pubescence persistent, particularly below. Inflorescence buds in winter not seen, but presumably large. Flowers (in the only raceme seen) were 17 in number, appearing with the leaves; rachis pubescent, 8 cm long; pedicels pubescent, to at least 3 cm; calyx pubescent; standard 2 cm or more broad, auricled, pubescent inside at the top, extending towards the base on either side of the blotch (figure 2.18c). In shape the flower parts are similar to those illustrated in figure 5.46. Legume not seen; seeds flattened, pale tan with fine black spotting (figure 5.42). Autumn colour yellow.

Figure 5.42   Seeds of *Wisteria brachybotrys*, collected wild

I expect to be able to expand this description when the seedling plants commence blooming. It will be particularly interesting to observe the size and shape of the inflorescence buds in winter and the variation in the number of flowers per raceme and its length. It appears, however, to resemble closely its cultivars, descriptions of which follow in this chapter. In all of these, as in the wild species, the breadth of the racemes results from the flowers being borne on pedicels up to 4.5 cm long.

According to Kawarada (1985) it occurs only in that part of Japan west and south of the Izu Peninsula on Honshu, and is known as 'Daruma Fuji' ('Wisteria from Mt Daruma') as well as 'Yama Fuji'. Other names encountered for this wisteria are 'No Fuji' ('Wild Wisteria'), also occasionally applied to *W. floribunda*, 'Fukuro Fuji' ('Bag Wisteria'), perhaps on account of the use of the fibre for making bags, and 'Kapitan Fuji'.

'Kapitan' is an old word derived from the Portuguese and used for the captains of European ships and for foreign officials in the early days of contact with the West. How it came to be used for this wisteria is a mystery, but Japanese authors (Tsukamoto 1984); Kawarada 1985) indicate that the original Chinese characters for the name are transliterated as 'ka-bi-tan' and mean 'flower-beautiful-short', which certainly sounds appropriate whatever the truth of the matter is. Perhaps, then, the use of the word 'kapitan' is just a mistake, but Kawarada says that the plant remained rare in cultivation throughout the Edo Period and suggests that the word was used to indicate this rarity. While it would be convenient and appropriate to call it 'Kabitan Fuji', the name 'Kapitan' is now so firmly entrenched in Japanese and other nurseries' lists, particularly in relation to the names of the cultivars, that it would be foolish not to go along with it.

CULTIVARS

In view of the frequent occurrence and ambiguity of names such as 'Alba', 'Rosea' and 'Violacea', together with the recommendation of the Code that Latin names no longer be given to cultivars, I have decided to use romanisations of the cultivar names favoured by Japanese horticulturalists and nurseries. Whether my suggestions will be followed remains to be seen. As many people are unaware of or choose to disregard the Code and to burden plants with infelicitous names which 'sell', I expect resistance.

'Aka Kapitan', 'Akebono', 'Alborosea'

See 'Showa Beni'.

'Alba', 'Alba Plena'

See 'Shiro Kapitan'.

'Murasaki Kapitan'   Figure 5.43

This cannot be confused with any other cultivar as it twines clockwise. It also differs in having the leaflets narrower and less densely pubescent, and the inflorescence buds in winter smaller, 6–8 mm × 5–7 mm, and rounded. The flowers are blue-violet in racemes of 35–47, strongly scented; floral bracts purple; rachis 14–22 cm; pedicels green, sometimes tinged mauve; inner surface of the standard pubescent at the top and down the sides of the blotch, outer pubescent around the claw and sometimes up the mid-line. The large velvety legumes become brownish and contain 2–4 dark reddish brown seeds, very faintly speckled with black (figure 5.18). The leaves turn a soft yellow in autumn and fall earlier than those of the other cultivars. Also while it blooms at the same time as the other cultivars in areas with cold winters, in mild climates, such as that of coastal New South Wales, it blooms a week or two earlier. Presumably it requires less exposure to cold to break its dormancy.

Figure 5.43   *Wisteria brachybotrys*
'Murasaki Kapitan'

The above description applies to the plant known as *W. venusta* f. *violacea* and *W. venusta* 'Violacea' and supplied by Japanese nurseries as 'Yama Fuji' and *W. brachybotrys* 'Murasaki Kapitan'. It is certainly not the 'Yama Fuji' as it occurs wild and is an anomalous plant since, while it resembles the wild form and the other cultivars in its general appearance, it twines in the opposite direction, has leaves with narrower, less-pubescent leaflets, smaller, rounded inflorescence buds, longer racemes with more flowers, and some pubescence on the outside of the standard. Perhaps it is just a horticulturally superior form which happens to twine in the opposite direction. On the other hand it may be of hybrid origin with some admixture of *W. floribunda*, which would account for the direction of twining, smaller winter buds, longer racemes, pubescence on the outside of the standard and perhaps its earlier blooming in mild climates. According to Uehara (1961) it was found in Hanado.

Whether this plant is what Siebold introduced to Ghent in 1830 or whether that was a wild form is not known. Nor is it known what the plant named *W. venusta* f. *violacea* by Rehder (1926) really was. Hence it seems reasonable to avoid the name 'Violacea' or even 'Venusta Violacea' for this cultivar and to opt for 'Murasaki Kapitan' ('Purple Kapitan').

Whatever its origin it is an excellent garden plant, blooming early in the season. I have obtained plants as 'Yama Fuji', 'Murasaki Kapitan' and *W. venusta* 'Violacea'. The last-mentioned came from the J. Clarke Nursery Company in 1963 and seems a little different from the others. On young plants the emerging leaves are paler, slightly distorted and weakly mottled, symptoms indicating a virus infection. As the plants mature these symptoms disappear. According to Wyman (1961), W. B. Clarke said that older plants, especially those grown in standard form, have an extraordinary profusion of bloom, better than any form of *W. sinensis*. My experience confirms this opinion.

'Okayama' Figure 5.44

Generally resembling 'Shiro Kapitan' as described in detail below. Equally strongly scented but differing in having darker inflorescence buds in winter, mauve floral bracts, pedicels and calyx, and soft pinkish mauve flowers, each with a large white blotch extending almost to the top of the standard. Kawarada (1985) suggests it may be a hybrid between 'Showa Beni' and 'Murasaki Kapitan'. Like the other forms of *W. brachybotrys* it blooms early in the season, although in areas with mild winters, such as coastal New South Wales, it blooms later than both *W. sinensis* and *W. floribunda* and their cultivars, in fact about the same time as *W. frutescens*. It seems probable that

this is because it takes longer in such climates for it to be subjected to an amount of low temperature sufficient to break its dormancy.

Presumably it originates from Okayama and it is sometimes called 'Okayama Issai'. However since it does not seem to differ from other cultivars of *W. brachybotrys* with regard to earliness of maturity, there seems to be little point in enlarging its name by adding the word 'Issai'. It is an interesting colour variant and worth growing for that reason.

'Plena'

See 'Shiro Kapitan'.

'Shira Fuji'

See 'Shiro Kapitan'.

'Shirobana Yama Fuji'

See 'Shiro Kapitan'.

Figure 5.44 *Wisteria brachybotrys* 'Okayama'

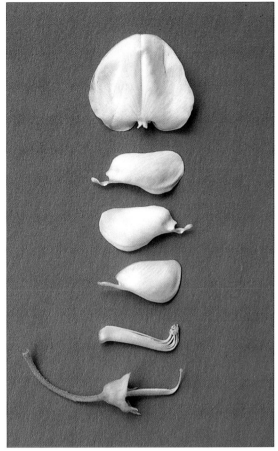

Figure 5.45 *Wisteria brachybotrys* 'Shiro Kapitan'

Figure 5.46 *Wisteria brachybotrys* 'Shiro Kapitan', flower structure

'Shiro Kapitan'   **Figures 5.40, 5.41, 5.45**

Vigorous deciduous climber, twining anticlockwise. Leaves with 9–13 leaflets, pale golden green when young, sometimes tinged bronze, densely and shortly pubescent above and below, pubescence persistent, particularly below. Inflorescence buds in winter pointed, 12–17 mm × 6–10 mm, outer two bracts dark brown, shortly hairy, inner bracts densely silky, golden. Flowers white, in racemes of 20–35, appearing with the leaves, strongly and sweetly scented; floral bracts large pale golden green; rachis stout, green, pubescent, 12–18 cm long; pedicels to 4.5 cm, pale greenish yellow, pubescent; calyx pubescent, greenish white, stained violet between the lobes at first; standard 2.0–2.8 cm broad, auricled, yellow at the base when newly opened, pubescent on the inner surface at the top and down to the base on either side of the blotch, outer surface glabrous; wings pure white, shortly auricled; keel pure white, with a short broad auricle, broadly rounded at the apex (figure 5.46). Pods velvety. Summer flowers tinged with pink. Autumn colour poor, leaves late falling.

This is the original *W. venusta* of Rehder and Wilson. Easy to grow, it is a first-rate garden plant, superior in colour to the white cultivars of *W. sinensis* and, like them, useful on account of its commencing to bloom about a fortnight before the white form of *W. floribunda*. However, like 'Okayama' and 'Showa Beni' it blooms late in areas with mild winters.

I have found it difficult to decide which cultivar name to favour. The old name 'Shira Fuji', 'White Wisteria', is confusing as there are other white wisterias. Sometimes it is called 'Shirobana Yama Fuji' ('White-flowered Mountain Wisteria'), but I prefer the Japanese practice of calling it 'Shiro Kapitan', usually translated as 'White Sea Captain'.

Kawarada (1985) says that it used to be found wild but that this is now very rare, adding that it was also rarely seen in cultivation in the Edo Period (1600–1853), which may account for its not being mentioned by Kaempfer, Thunberg or Siebold. He says, too, that, presumably because it blooms as a young plant, it is often sold for planting together with 'Issai Fuji' ('Domino') for contrasting colour. This may explain why these two plants have sometimes been listed as 'Prematura Alba' and 'Prematura' respectively.

From time to time a double white form is claimed to exist. According to Bean (1932) this appears to have been in cultivation in Britain previous to the introduction of the single type as *W. chinensis alba plena*. On the basis of a specimen sent by Bean it was described as *W. venusta* f. *plena* by Rehder and Wilson, who noted that, as far as they knew, it was the only white double-flowered wisteria in cultivation.

As far as I can ascertain, no double white form is known in Japan and the only plants I have seen labelled as the double form have produced single flowers. Similarly Wyman (1961) says that all plants received under the name *W. venusta plena* turned out to be *W. floribunda* 'Violacea Plena'. However in the description given in *Curtis's Botanical Magazine* (Prain 1919) it is stated that the flowers are frequently more or less double, though this is not shown in the plate. And I have a report of a late raceme with more or less double flowers produced at Cannington Court, Somerset, in 1992 by a plant which

earlier had produced only single blooms at its main flowering. So perhaps the ordinary white form occasionally produces double flowers and that is all there is to it.

It seems likely that it is on the basis of the name *W. chinensis alba plena* that Japanese authors (for example, Uehara 1961) have listed 'Shirobana Yae Shina Fuji' ('White-flowered Double Chinese Wisteria'), which one might expect to refer to this occasional aberration in 'Shiro Kapitan'.

'Showa Beni'   Figures 5.47 and on page 153

Generally resembling 'Shiro Kapitan' and blooming about the same time, early in cold areas and late in mild. Differing in having darker inflorescence buds in winter, greenish gold floral bracts tinged with pink, pinkish purple pedicels and calyx, the standard very pale mauve-pink inside with a small yellow blotch, darker outside, wings and keel mauve-pink, darker, particularly the keel towards the apex, and the scent faint. The summer flowers are a more uniform mauve-pink with a scarcely noticeable blotch.

In Japan it is also listed as 'Akebono' ('Dawn') or 'Akebono Kapitan', 'Aka Kapitan' ('Red Sea Captain') and 'Alborosea'. 'Akebono' is an overused word and is sometimes applied to the *W. floribunda* cultivar 'Kuchibeni', as is 'Alborosea'.

Figure 5.47   *Wisteria brachybotrys* 'Showa Beni'

'Aka Kapitan' is a name which makes it clear that it is a cultivar of *W. brachybotrys*, but I feel it is wise to avoid re-using the word 'Kapitan' if an acceptable alternative name is available. This leaves 'Showa Beni' ('Red of the Showa Period'), a more mellifluous name which tells us something of the plant's origin.

Kawarada (1985) states that it is occasionally found growing naturally, though now very rarely. Presumably it arose or was introduced to cultivation in the Showa Period. Anyway it has only been listed in Japanese catalogues in recent years. It is undoubtedly the most nearly pink wisteria introduced to date and should prove a useful addition to gardens, particularly since it blooms earlier in the season than *W. floribunda* 'Honbeni' in cold climates and later in mild ones.

'Violacea'

See 'Murasaki Kapitan'.

'Yae Kapitan'

Just as claims have been made for the existence of a double white cultivar, so in Japan the existence of a double violet form has been reported. Kawarada (1985) says that it is one of the few double wisterias, very difficult to obtain, and that it would be sad if it became extinct. He says that its racemes are 10–15 cm long and that its garden name is 'Yae Kapitan' ('Double Sea Captain'). If it exists it should be worth propagating and reintroducing.

W. japonica Sieb. & Zucc.

This plant is dealt with in chapter 7 as *Millettia japonica* (Sieb. & Zucc.) A. Gray.

Other species

W. nipponica

Stritch (1984), as mentioned earlier, has proposed a new genus, *Rehsonia*, for the Asiatic species at present included in *Wisteria*. At the same time he published the name of a new species, *Rehsonia nipponica* Stritch, designating as the type a specimen, 6579 (A), collected by E. H. Wilson on 27 April 1914, near Tokyo. It is described as twining anticlockwise, having leaves with 9–13 leaflets, glabrous at maturity, and racemes 15–20 cm long, with showy blue, violet or white flowers having standards 2.1–2.2 cm broad.

This description appears to fit *W. sinensis,* so an examination of Wilson's specimen would be necessary in order to decide whether there is any justification for describing it as a new species.

W. nipponicola Makino
AZUMA FUJI

This is listed by Uehara (1961), who says it was found by Dr Makino in the mountains near Hanno, Saitama, in 1948. 'Azuma' means 'east' in the sense of the eastern provinces of Japan, that is, where Tokyo is situated. Uehara goes on to record that, in the September 1956 issue of the periodical *Nogusa,* Dr Hieyama reported that he had discovered a wisteria in Zoshigaya, Tokyo, which was different from any known type. Uehara also mentions that there is, or was, a plant owned by Mr Nakane in Shinjuku, Tokyo, which is thirty years old and flowers five times a year.

What all this means is unclear, to say the least. I have been unable to track down anything further about *W. nipponicola,* which does not seem to have been heard of again.

CHAPTER 6

Hybrids and Cultivars of Unknown Provenance

Among the wisterias in cultivation are a number which do not seem able, at least as yet, to be reliably assigned to a particular species. It seems probable that at least some of them are hybrids. Those that have come to my attention are described below.

'Burford'   Figure 6.2

This has been introduced by the Mears Ashby Nurseries, Northamptonshire, England, as a cultivar of *W. floribunda*. While in general it exhibits the characteristics of that species, it shows differences which suggest that it may be of hybrid origin. Hence I have included it in this chapter.

'Burford' twines clockwise and has broad, bold foliage with 13 leaflets. The racemes are up to 41 cm long, some probably longer, with up to 84 or more flowers; scent sweet, not musky; pedicels green, tinged mauve; calyx greyish violet, shading to white at the lobes; standard 2.5 cm broad, pale violet, pubescent at the top inside and around the claw outside; wings and keel darker.

As only half the flowers were open on the racemes at the only time I was able to examine them, they would undoubtedly have become longer. The individual flowers are larger than normally encountered in *W. floribunda* and because of this, together with its vigour, its bold foliage, and its sweet scent, it is tempting to suggest that this handsome plant is a hybrid between *W. floribunda* and *W. sinensis*. It is very similar to 'Lavender Lace', described below, and should prove a valuable addition to our gardens.

Figure 6.1   *Wisteria* 'Lavender Lace'

Figure 6.2 *Wisteria* 'Burford'

Figure 6.3 *Wisteria* 'Caroline'

A chromosome count of these plants might prove informative, as perhaps their vigour and flower size may be the result of polyploidy rather than hybridity.

'Caroline'   Figure 6.3

This early blooming cultivar has become quite well known in New Zealand, whence it has begun to be distributed. According to a letter written by Professor Vernon Stoutmeyer to Mr Trevor Davies of Pakuranga, New Zealand, it was introduced by the late William H. Chandler, one time Dean of Agriculture at the University of California, Los Angeles, somewhere about 1952 or 1953, and named for his wife. Professor Stoutmeyer added that many plants were sold locally.

While it sometimes is listed as a cultivar of *W. sinensis* or as a hybrid, it exhibits the general

characteristics of *W. floribunda*. It twines clockwise and the leaves have 13–15 narrow leaflets, pale bronze when young. The racemes are 17.5–21.0 cm long, held horizontally for a start, becoming pendulous, with 89–105 violet flowers; scent faint; floral bracts long-pointed, pale green suffused mauve; pedicels 1.5–1.7 cm, purple, pubescent; calyx greyish mauve, grading to white at the lobes, shortly pubescent; standard 1.8–2.0 cm broad, pale violet, pubescent at the top inside, glabrous outside, the blotch green at its base, grading to yellow then white above; wings and keel a little darker. Pods and seeds not seen. Autumn colour good, leaves falling at about the same time as those of the *W. floribunda* cultivars.

'Caroline' blooms early, often a little before *W. brachybotrys* and *W. sinensis,* and is thus useful for adding variety at the beginning of the season. But apart from this and the horizontal disposition of the young racemes as in 'Formosa', I can see no reason to assume that it is anything other than a form of *W. floribunda* with short racemes and very closely spaced flowers, more densely packed even than in *W. floribunda* 'Geisha'.

'Child's Ever-Blooming'

Listed in the past by Duncan and Davies, New Plymouth, New Zealand, as 'Short thick deep purple'. Perhaps not a true wisteria. It seems to have disappeared, at least under this name.

'Formosa'   Figures 6.4, 9.2

According to Rehder (1922), who first described this plant, it originated at Holm Lea, Brookline, Massachusetts, about 1905 from a seed of *W. floribunda* 'Alba' ('Shiro Noda') planted by Charles Sander and apparently fertilised by pollen of *W. sinensis*, flowering simultaneously in the greenhouse. A plant bearing this name was obtained in 1963 from the J. Clarke Nursery Company, San Jose, and is described as follows.

Vigorous climber with bold foliage, twining clockwise, the leaves with 11–15 broad leaflets, pale bronze when young. Racemes 26–35 cm long, with 73–86 flowers; scent medium; rachis dark purplish green, pubescent; floral bracts purplish; pedicels 1.5–2.2 cm, purplish, pubescent; calyx purple, greenish white at the lobes, pubescent; standard 1.7–2.1 cm broad, violet, pubescent at the top inside and around the claw outside, blotch very distinct, yellow, edged white; wings and keel darker. Legumes thick, 9.0–21.5 cm long, with 1–6 large seeds, dark reddish brown, finely speckled black (figure 5.18). Autumn colour poor, leaves late falling as in *W. sinensis*. The inflorescence buds in winter are 5.0–7.5 mm × 3.0 mm, the two outer bracts dark reddish brown, sparsely hairy, the inner ones shortly silky-hairy, slightly exposed.

In its general characteristics it certainly does seem to be a hybrid with the parentage claimed for it. Its appearance is coarser than that of *W. floribunda*, the pods are thicker, the leaflets are broader, and the leaves are lost later, as with *W. sinensis*. However the leaves have more leaflets than that species and the individual flowers, appearing later in the season, are smaller, very similar to those of *W. floribunda*. Another characteristic feature is that, as with 'Caroline', the young racemes are held more or less horizontally, becoming pendulous as the flowers open.

I cannot agree with Rehder that it is superior to both presumed parents, but it certainly is distinctive, a good deep colour, and comparatively late blooming.

Figure 6.4 *Wisteria* 'Formosa'

'Issai'

The claim has been made by Wyman (1949, 1961) that 'Issai' twines in both directions and thus may be a hybrid. Presumably it is on the basis of this statement that some people have listed it under *W. × formosa* on the assumption, for which there is no evidence, that it is a hybrid of *W. floribunda* and *W. sinensis*. It is not possible now to know what the plant described by Wyman as 'Issai' actually was, and the author's examination of all plants, other than *W. brachybotrys* 'Okayama Issai', with 'Issai' as all or part of the name has indicated that they twine clockwise only and exhibit the characteristics of *W. floribunda*, the species to which they are considered to belong by the Japanese. Hence I have included them as cultivars of that species in chapter 5.

'Lavender Lace'   Figure 6.1

This name has been given to a plant originating in Brooklands Park, New Plymouth, New Zealand. It is a large-flowered wisteria which twines clockwise and has leaves with 13–15 leaflets, pale bronze-green when young. The racemes are up to 50 cm long with 83–108 flowers; scent sweet, not musky; floral bracts pale green, suffused mauve; pedicels up to 3.3 cm, green, suffused violet at either end; standard 2.4–2.5 cm broad, pale violet, pubescent at the top inside and around the claw outside; wings and keel darker. Autumn colour quite good.

It is very similar to 'Burford' and is worthy of general cultivation. It is suggested that it, too, may be a hybrid between *W. floribunda* and *W. sinensis*.

'Mrs McCullagh'

I have not seen this; perhaps it is now lost to cultivation. Wyman (1949, 1961) says it is not a true *W. floribunda* type, twining by climbing from left to right (anticlockwise), and probably a hybrid of *W. sinensis*. He (1961) describes it as having clusters six inches [15.2 cm]; moderate fragrance; color only noted as bluish-violet. It is less vigorous than the others; not a good type.' Should it turn up anywhere its qualities might perhaps be reassessed.

'Texas Purple'   Figure 6.5

According to the Monrovia Nursery Company of California this cultivar has replaced *W. floribunda* 'Royal Purple' in their propagation schedule because of its ability to flower at a very young age in containers. It originally came from the Verhalen Nursery in Texas.

Although 'Texas Purple' is described as a cultivar of *W. floribunda,* in the photograph provided the flowers appear similar to those of *W. sinensis*. Because of this and its precocious blooming it has been included in this chapter. When careful comparisons can be carried out it may be possible to assign it to a species with certainty.

Figure 6.5 *Wisteria* 'Texas Purple' (Monrovia Nursery Company)

Figure 6.6   *Wisteria* no. 8,
Cannington College

Figure 6.7   Presumed hybrid between
W. brachybotrys and *W. floribunda*

'Zealandia'

This was listed by Duncan and Davies as a New Zealand raised variety with pretty blue flowers with a yellow eye and yellowish foliage. Along with 'Child's Ever-Blooming' this, too, seems to have disappeared. The mention of yellowish foliage suggests that it may have been a form of *W. brachybotrys*.

UNNAMED SEEDLINGS

In the National Wisteria Collection at Cannington College, Somerset, are two large-flowered plants very similar to 'Burford' and 'Lavender Lace'. These appear to have arisen from grafted plants where the seedling stock has outgrown the scion.

The plant labelled 'No. 8' has soft mauve flowers (figure 6.6), while that labelled 'F' is darker and more nearly violet. Both these plants seem to me to be candidates for propagation and distribution.

Somewhat similar is a wisteria which arose from the rootstock of a plant I obtained from the Arnold Arboretum as *W. floribunda* 'Alba' (figure 6.7). This twines clockwise, is very vigorous, and has leaves with 9–15 broad leaflets. It blooms early with racemes 26–32 cm with 59–79 pale blue-violet flowers on pedicels 1.5–3.0 cm long. The standard is 2.2–2.5 cm broad and is markedly pubescent inside at the top, the hairs running some distance down the sides and down the upper borders of the blotch. Again the scent is strong and sweet, not musky as is usual in *W. floribunda*. The broad leaflets, early flowering, sweet scent, large flowers, and pubescence of the standard suggest that it may be a hybrid of *W. brachybotrys* and *W. floribunda.*

Another plant worth mentioning was obtained from the J. Clarke Nursery Company in 1963 as 'Issai' but appears to be another example of the rootstock having outgrown the scion. It twines clockwise, is very vigorous, and has leaves with 9–15 large broad leaflets. The racemes are typical of *W. floribunda* and are 30–36 cm long with 87–101 pale blue-violet flowers (figure 6.8). The

standard is 2.0–2.1 cm broad, pubescent at the top inside and on the claw outside, and the scent is faint. The autumn colour is poor and the leaves are shed very late, as with *W. sinensis.* The legumes are unusually thick and rounded, as in 'Formosa', with 2–7 pinkish tan seeds, very heavily spotted and blotched with black (figure 5.18). It is an excellent garden plant, early blooming, floriferous, and of a similar colour to the *W. floribunda* cultivars 'Geisha' and 'Lawrence'. It was illustrated on the cover of *The Garden,* volume 116, part 2, February 1991.

I have raised other plants of apparently hybrid origin from seed collected from cultivated plants of '*W. venusta* Rehd. & Wils.' in Shanghai (Shanghai Botanic Garden Seed List 1984, no. 591). These bear little resemblance to *W. venusta* (*W. brachybotrys* 'Shiro Kapitan'), twining clockwise, having leaves with 9–17 narrowly ovate to elliptic leaflets, differing little in pubescence from either *W. floribunda* or *W. sinensis.*

Only two have bloomed at the time of writing, one (figure 6.9) with pale bronze young leaves and 14–30 cm racemes, some of them branched, bearing 50–115 small, somewhat deformed, faintly scented, violet flowers; floral bracts small, purplish, pubescent; rachis green, sparsely pubescent; pedicels to 2.7 cm, green tinged purple, pubescent; calyx violet, pubescent; standard usually divided, narrow, to 1.8 cm tall, pubescent on the top inner surface, marked yellow at the base; wings and keel darker. Autumn colour poor, leaves falling much earlier than those of *W. brachybotrys.* Floral buds in winter conspicuous, 7 mm × 5 mm, rounded at the apex.

The other (figure 6.10) has pale green young leaves and white, faintly scented flowers, 65–85 in racemes 22–30 cm long; floral bracts small, green tinged purple, pubescent; rachis green, sparsely pubescent; pedicels to 3 cm, pale green, pubescent; calyx white, tinged purplish green

Figure 6.8   Blue wisteria with hybrid characteristics at Nooroo, Mount Wilson, NSW

Figure 6.9 Hybrid wisteria raised
from seed from Shanghai

Figure 6.10 Hybrid wisteria raised
from seed from Shanghai

towards the pedicel, pubescent, lowest lobe long-pointed; standard a little taller than broad, 1.8 cm in diameter, white, marked yellow at the base, pubescent at the top on the inner face, otherwise glabrous; wings white, faintly tinged violet at the apex; keel white, violet at the apex. Autumn colour good, leaves falling much earlier than those of *W. brachybotrys*. Floral buds in winter conspicuous, 7 mm × 5 mm, rounded.

These plants are very distinctive. In their direction of twining, number of leaflets per leaf, time of leaf fall and length of raceme they show a much greater similarity to *W. floribunda* than to either *W. brachybotrys* or *W. sinensis*. The inflorescence buds in winter, however, are much larger and are similar to those of *W. brachybotrys* 'Murasaki Kapitan'. Perhaps these seedlings are hybrids of *W. brachybotrys* 'Shiro Kapitan' and *W. floribunda*. The white-flowered one is very similar to a specimen in the herbarium at Kew labelled *W. brevidentata,* no. 1291 (see chapter 5).

Of supposed similar parentage is a plant introduced by Chiba University, which I saw at Mr Kawarada's nursery. It is claimed to be a hybrid between *W. floribunda* 'Honbeni' and *W. brachybotrys* 'Showa Beni'. It had not yet flowered but in its vegetative characteristics it appeared close to *W. floribunda*.

127

CHAPTER 7

Summer Wisterias

In addition to the plants described in the foregoing chapters, there are a number of others included in the Japanese concept of 'fuji' and which turn up from time to time with wisterias in lists, catalogues and other writings. Also in Australia there are plants that were originally described as species of *Wisteria* before being transferred to other genera subsequently. While all these have much in common with the species dealt with so far, they show greater similarity to members of the genus *Millettia* Wight & Arn., in which have been included some 150 species of trees, shrubs and climbers, nearly all of which are evergreen and native to the tropics and subtropics.

The genus *Millettia* itself is a heterogeneous assemblage and it and other members of the legume tribe Millettieae have been reviewed by Geesink (1984). It is Geesink's view that there is a number of *Millettia* species with truly paniculate inflorescences which would be more satisfactorily accommodated in the genus *Callerya*. The *Millettia* species described below are in this category but, while Schot (1994) has incorporated nineteen species in *Callerya*, including *M. reticulata* and the Australian species, she has excluded *M. japonica*, as mentioned in Chapter 1. So it seemed simplest for the purposes of this book to leave the species included here in *Millettia* for the time being, as the application of modern techniques, including DNA sequencing, may well lead to further changes. Also, since only a few species are involved, they have not been described in alphabetical order but in a sequence which reflects their relationships.

Figure 7.1 *Millettia japonica*

Millettia japonica (Sieb. & Zucc.) A. Gray

Figure 7.1

NATSU FUJI

This plant was brought to the notice of the outside world when it was described by Siebold and Zuccarini (1835–41) as *Wisteria japonica*. Siebold waxed lyrical about it, saying that at the time of flowering, in July and August, the racemes of white flowers which hang from the tree tops, provide a magnificent coup-d'oeil and give the shrubs they cover an air of wild beauty, which is highly esteemed especially in Japan, where people love to imitate in cultivation its natural profusion. Well that may have been so in Siebold's time, but today the plant is rarely seen in cultivation in Japan or anywhere else.

Bean (1980) records that it was introduced for Veitch by Maries in 1878. Wilson (1916) reported that so far it had proved disappointing in the gardens of Europe and North America, and Rehder (1927) notes that it is less showy than the other wisterias he describes. This is not surprising as, with its small, greenish white flowers borne among the expanded foliage (figure 7.1), it is hard to imagine it creating any sort of coup-d'oeil. However it may be that there are conditions under which it produces flowers profusely enough to create such an effect, particularly were a large number of terminal inflorescences to be formed.

Siebold and Zuccarini gave as its Japanese names 'Ko-fudsi' ('Small Wisteria') and 'Saru-fudsi' ('Monkey Wisteria'), but nowadays 'Natsu Fuji' ('Summer Wisteria') seems to be the name most frequently used, though Ohwi (1965) gives 'Doyo Fuji' ('Midsummer Wisteria') as an alternative.

Although this plant was originally described as a *Wisteria* and is deciduous, its flowers are produced in summer in leafless axillary racemes and terminal panicles and resemble those of *Millettia* or *Callerya* rather than those of *Wisteria*. The description which follows is based on plants imported from Japan in 1990.

Vigorous, slender, deciduous climber, twining clockwise. Leaves with 9–15 leaflets, pale bronze-green when young, shortly pubescent on the veins below, glabrous above, becoming deep green, slightly bullate and somewhat glossy; leaflets ovate to narrowly ovate, usually 1.5–5.0 cm long, 1–2 cm wide, but up to 12 cm long and 4.5 cm wide on strong shoots; rachis, petiolules and midribs tinged reddish. Flowers in racemes of up to 90 or more, axillary or in terminal panicles on the current season's growth, appearing in summer well after the leaves; peduncle short, not leafy; rachis reddish, shortly pubescent; pedicels up to 5 mm, reddish, almost glabrous; calyx about 4 mm long, glabrous or only slightly pubescent, cup-shaped, pale green, teeth short, broadly triangular, tinged with red; standard glabrous, not auricled, 8–10 mm broad and tall, greenish white with a pronounced greenish yellow blotch; wings glabrous, shortly auricled, rounded at the apex, not joined, narrowly ovate to oblong, about 11 mm long; keel elements glabrous, each with a very small broadly triangular auricle, rounded at the apex, about 12 mm long; stamens 10, glabrous, 9 joined, 1 free; ovary and style glabrous, early becoming tinged with red; young legumes reddish brown (figure 7.2). I could detect no scent but it may be that it becomes scented under different conditions, perhaps at night.

In Japan this species blooms in July–August and in Sydney, Australia, from mid-January to early February. It is native to the more southern and warmer parts of Japan and so presumably it is less cold-hardy than the true wisterias of that country. It has also been recorded from South Korea, but whether it is native there or introduced is unclear. Rehder and Wilson (1916) record its collection from the grounds of a temple in Fusan (Pusan?) by Professor Sargent in 1903.

It would appear that there are two cultivars, and these are described below.

'Hichirimen'

A plant with this name, sometimes spelled 'Highirimen', is distributed by Otto Eisenhut, of San Nazzaro, Switzerland. It was apparently imported by Sir Peter Smithers for his garden at Vico Morcote and is stated to be yellow flowered. I have imported a plant which has not yet bloomed but it certainly closely resembles *M. japonica*. However it differs from the wild type described above in twining anticlockwise and having leaves shortly pubescent above and below. It is expected that further observation of this plant in cultivation will clarify the matter.

Whether the above spelling of the cultivar name is correct or whether, even, it is correct to apply it to this plant I do not know. However it does seem odd that I have also encountered the name 'Hichirimen' as a cultivar of *W. floribunda* (see chapter 5). But having got used to the ways of the horticultural world nothing surprises me.

Without seeing the name written in the original characters it is impossible to know what 'Hichirimen' means or indicates. 'Chirimen' is the Japanese word for a kind of crêpe fabric, so perhaps it has something to do with this.

'Hime Fuji'   Figure 7.3

This dwarf form remains shrubby, but when it produces the occasional climbing shoot it twines clockwise. The leaves are densely packed, smaller than in the wild type, with 9–11 narrow, shortly pubescent leaflets, not as glossy as in the wild type, nor do they show any tendency to become bullate. Ohwi (1965) says it is a non-flowering cultivar and in my experience this is certainly the case. In Japan it is usually grown as a pot plant.

It is also sometimes listed as 'Mekura Fuji' ('Blind Wisteria'), wrongly spelled on occasions

Figure 7.2 *Millettia japonica*, flower structure

Figure 7.3 *Millettia japonica* 'Hime Fuji'

as 'Mekwa Fuji', as well as 'Microphylla', 'Nana', or even as *W. floribunda* 'Nana'. As mentioned in chapter 4, it seems likely that the plant called *W. sinensis* 'Nankingensis' belongs here too. Until some reason is put forward for doing otherwise, I suggest that this cultivar be left with its Japanese name 'Hime Fuji' ('Dwarf Wisteria').

Millettia sp.   Figure 7.4

CLOSE TO *M. JAPONICA*

Among the *Wisteria* specimens at Kew is one collected by George Forrest, labelled 'No. 24130, fragrant, pure white, on cliffs and side valleys, 8000 feet [2438 m], Yunnan, May 1924.' No locality is given. The specimen bears racemes up to 30 cm long, grouped as a panicle, and resembles a larger and more showy *M. japonica*. The leaves, however, have only five leaflets, glabrous above and sparsely pubescent below. It would appear to be a plant worthy of cultivation.

In 1992 the Australian collectors Simon Goodwin and Robert Cherry found a similar plant, also with leaves of five leaflets, at two localities at 2000 m on Fan Si Pan, Vietnam's highest mountain, close to the Yunnan border almost due south of Mengzi. It is now in cultivation in Australia.

It is a vigorous evergreen climber, twining anticlockwise. Leaves very variable in size, with 5 ovate to elliptic leaflets, 5–16 cm long, glabrous above and shortly pubescent below, at least when young, becoming leathery, deep green, glossy and somewhat bullate at maturity. When it blooms it will be interesting to see whether it is the same as Forrest's plant.

Millettia reticulata Benth.   Figure 7.5

MURASAKI NATSU FUJI

Whereas the plants described above could, at least in the vegetative state, be confused with true *Wisteria* species, this evergreen vine from Taiwan and southern China is quite distinct. Its vernacular name means 'Purple Summer Wisteria', and in Japan it is usually grown as a pot plant. While it has a quiet charm, it seems unlikely, since its flowers are small and produced only over a short period annually, that it will become a popular garden plant. It blooms at the same time as *M. japonica*.

Figure 7.4 *Millettia* sp., North Vietnam

Figure 7.5 *Millettia reticulata* (Murasaki Natsu Fuji)

Figure 7.6   *Millettia* sp. (Satsuma Sakuko Fuji)

It is a slender evergreen climber, twining clockwise. Leaves with 5–9 leaflets, yellowish green when young; leaflets broadly elliptic, leathery, shortly pubescent above and below when young, hairs on the upper surface dark, becoming sparse. Flowers small, violet, with no detectable scent, up to 90 or more in axillary racemes and terminal panicles; rachis green, shortly pubescent, up to 12 cm; pedicels green, pubescent, 2–3 mm long; calyx cup-shaped, green, pubescent towards the pedicel, the lobes purple, short and broadly triangular; standard glabrous, not auricled, 8–9 mm broad and tall with a conspicuous, greenish yellow blotch; wings not joined, rounded at their apices, each with a short, triangular auricle; keel elements with no obvious auricle, rounded at the apex; stamens 10, 9 fused, 1 free; ovary and style glabrous. This species has recently been transferred to *Callerya* by Schot (1994).

Millettia sp.   Figure 7.6

SATSUMA SAKUKO FUJI

So far I have not been able to locate the correct specific epithet for this species. However, whatever it is, the plant is undoubtedly a candidate for transfer to *Callerya*. The vernacular name means 'Red-flowering Wisteria from Satsuma'. It is cultivated in Japan for its dark reddish purple flowers which appear later in the season than those of all other plants known as Fuji. In Sydney it blooms from late January to mid-February. Since the name Satsuma Sakuko Fuji appears from time to time in Japanese lists and catalogues, this has sometimes been wrongly interpreted as indicating that a red-flowered wisteria exists. Also, the name is occasionally transliterated as Satsuma Sakko Fuji.

Like *M. reticulata* it is an evergreen climber, twining clockwise. Leaves with 3–7 leaflets, pale yellowish green when young; leaflets narrowly elliptic, leathery, shortly pubescent above and below on emergence, becoming almost glabrous. Flowers deep reddish purple with no detectable scent, densely packed in axillary racemes and terminal panicles; rachis up to 10 cm, sometimes more, green, pubescent; pedicels green, pubescent, 6–7 mm long; calyx suffused reddish purple, broadly cup-shaped, glabrous, about 3 mm long, with very short, broadly triangular lobes; standard 1.3–1.4 cm tall, 1.0–1.1 cm broad, glabrous, not auricled, with a small but conspicuous greenish yellow blotch; wings narrowly ovate to oblong, with a short auricle, rounded at their apices, not joined, shorter than the keel; keel blunt, more or less oblong, not noticeably auricled; stamens glabrous, 10, 9 joined, 1 free; ovary and style glabrous.

Millettia megasperma (F. Muell.) Benth.

Figures 7.7. 7.8

NATIVE WISTERIA

This Australian plant, native to the rainforests of northern New South Wales and Queensland, is included here because of its similarity to the species described above and because it is known locally as Native Wisteria. The specific epithet *megasperma* means 'large-seeded' and refers to the large chestnut-like seeds which it produces. It was originally described as *Wistaria megasperma* by Ferdinand von Mueller before being transferred to *Millettia* by Bentham (1864) in his *Flora Australiensis*. It is a handsome climber with larger individual flowers than the species described above, borne in much larger panicles. It is, of course, suitable only for mild climates, though it can tolerate some frost. In Sydney it blooms in October and November.

M. megasperma is a very vigorous evergreen climber, twining anticlockwise. Leaves with 7–13 leaflets, usually 11; leaflets glossy, elliptical, to 9 cm long, sparsely pubescent when young, becoming glabrous except on the midrib beneath. Flowers up to 100 or more in axillary racemes, usually grouped in large terminal panicles; floral bracts purple; rachis pale green, sometimes tinged with purple, pubescent, up to 15 cm long; pedicels pubescent, whitish, stained purple towards the calyx, 1.0–1.5 cm long; calyx campanulate, pubescent, whitish with purple lobes; standard 1.5–2.0 cm broad, whitish and shortly pubescent outside, violet within, with a greenish yellow blotch, pubescent at the top but otherwise glabrous; wings glabrous, deep purple, rounded at the apices, each with a pointed auricle above the claw; keel elements paler, dark towards the apex, glabrous, obtusely pointed and with a short triangular auricle above the claw; stamens glabrous, 9 joined, 1 free; ovary pubescent along its upper edge; style glabrous.

Although rarely seen in gardens there are another two similar Australian species. *M. australis* Benth., with the common name of Blunt Wisteria, occurs in the same region as *M. megasperma* and *M. pilipes* F. M. Bailey, which is known as Northern Wisteria, is found in the rainforests of northern Queensland. As mentioned earlier, all three Australian species of *Millettia* have now been transferred to *Callerya* by Schot (1994).

Other Australian leguminous climbers to have attracted the name 'wisteria' are the Native Derris, *Derris involuta* (Sprague) Sprague, another rainforest plant from north-east New South Wales and southern Queensland, and *Hardenbergia comptoniana* (Andrews) Benth., the Native Wisteria of south-western Western Australia.

Figure 7.7 *above* &
Figure 7.8 *left*
Millettia megasperma

CHAPTER 8

Cultivation

Establishment and general cultivation

Anyone who has grown wisterias probably thinks this chapter unnecessary. You just put them in and stand back, secateurs at the ready. In fact some people actually avoid planting wisterias, fearing they may overwhelm fences, trees or even the house. This is a pity, as sensible use of those secateurs will keep them under control and ensure prolific bloom.

It is necessary, obviously, to keep them watered after planting until they become established. Likewise, to get them to grow to the size you would like, applications of fertiliser in early spring and again in midsummer will hasten matters. After that it is rarely necessary to do anything other than prune them. No doubt because of the symbiotic associations with which their roots become involved (see chapter 2) they become largely self-sufficient, as they do in the wild. Needless to say, these generalisations apply to plants grown in the ground in reasonably moist temperate climates and in soils with passable levels of nutrients. Under harsher conditions, or in containers, regular applications of water and nutrients will be necessary. The plants themselves will let you know.

One frequently hears the complaint 'I can't get my wisteria to flower.' Well there are various possible explanations for this irksome state of affairs. Firstly, wisterias usually do not flower when young. Three to five years may pass before they commence. Secondly, they should be grown in full sun. Under natural conditions their growth habit ensures that they sprawl over trees, shrubs or rocks with their leaves in bright light, which seems to be a requirement for the abundant development of flower buds.

Figure 8.1   Wisteria pruning at Nishiarai Daishi, Tokyo

Thirdly, if they are given lots of water and fertiliser, they may devote their energy to growth rather than to the development of flower buds so, as mentioned before, once a plant is established it is best to do nothing to it unless it shows signs of distress. Finally, it is most important to prune correctly as described in the next section, as heavy pruning, particularly late in the growing season or in winter, is likely to remove those parts of the plant which would produce the next season's flowers.

Training and pruning

The Chinese Wisteria, *W. sinensis,* seems to bloom prolifically whatever you do to it and looks wonderful when allowed to climb trees in an uncontrolled manner, even though this can lead to trouble eventually. In most gardens, however, the best results are obtained by keeping it within bounds. It can be grown against walls, over fences, trained around verandahs, over arches, on pergolas, as a standard, as a shrub or as a bonsai.

After planting, the new season's long shoots should be tied back in the positions desired and unwanted shoots removed as they appear. Removal of the tips of the long shoots when they have reached the desired length will encourage the development of side shoots, which may then be treated similarly. Once the plant has reached the preferred size and shape, all new shoots should be cut back to two or three leaves at the base, rather than removing them altogether, as this encourages the development of the short spurs on which many of the flower buds appear. Any drastic shaping or cutting back should be carried out in spring, immediately after flowering. All suckers and unwanted shoots are most easily removed as they appear, as they come away easily when pulled or bent over while still young and soft.

Against walls the best results are obtained by positioning the lateral branches horizontally, either formally in the manner of an espalier or in a more relaxed manner, according to taste and circumstance. This ensures that the racemes will be well displayed (figures 8.2–8.4).

In order to train a plant as a standard it is necessary to provide it with a firm wooden or metal post. After planting, a single vigorous shoot should be tied to the support and allowed to climb to the top by twining. Once the top is reached this shoot should be carefully unwound and then tied to the support so that it twines around it once or one and a half times. If preferred it may be kept straight but the former system allows the plant to be self-supporting and gives it a more graceful appearance.

Once the shoot has grown to about 50 cm beyond the top of the support, remove the tip. Lateral branches usually then appear along the full length of the stem. It is wise not to remove these entirely for a start but merely to shorten each back to four or five leaves, allowing the lateral shoots at the top to grow as long as you wish. The plant is then left with plenty of leaves to photosynthesise and the young stem is protected from sun damage. After one or perhaps two years, when the upper branch system is well developed, the short branches on the lower part should be removed and the trunk kept free of side growths thereafter. Plants of all the Asian species trained in this manner are most ornamental whether in bloom or leaf (figures 1.2, 9.2 and on page 6).

The Chinese Wisteria is also most handsome when grown as a shrub (figures 4.21 and 4.29) and, while it may require staking for a start, it soon becomes self-supporting. It should be allowed to develop a branching system from the base and then be treated as described previously. As with the other systems of training it can be kept whatever size and shape is wished.

Figure 8.2   *Wisteria sinensis* at Montacute, Somerset

Figure 8.3   *Wisteria sinensis* and *Wisteria floribunda* at Magdalen College, Oxford

Figure 8.4   *Wisteria sinensis* at Montacute, Somerset

Figure 8.5 *Wisteria sinensis* shading an outlet of a popular international enterprise in Beijing

W. sinensis is most effective, too, when grown as a bonsai or penjing (figure 4.22). I have had no experience in the training and maintenance of such plants, but advice can be obtained from manuals on the subject or from experts.

Although this wisteria is frequently grown on a pergola, it is usually less effective than *W. floribunda* when displayed in this way, as the racemes are shorter and do not hang through in the same manner, except in the case of the longer-racemed forms seen in Beijing (figure 8.5).

The training and pruning of wisterias requires some effort in their early years, but on reaching maturity the production of new shoots lessens annually and the task becomes much less time-consuming. The plants soon assume picturesque forms, and much pleasure is to be gained from the shape and disposition of their trunks and branches, even in winter.

Old plants, or plants which have grown in an unwanted manner, may be rejuvenated by cutting them back drastically, almost to ground level if desired. Wisterias are almost impossible to kill.

While everything mentioned above applies equally to the Japanese *W. brachybotrys* and its cultivars, a little more care needs to be taken with *W. floribunda* to ensure that the flowers are produced and displayed satisfactorily. This species and its cultivars rarely produce their best effect when allowed to grow in an uncontrolled manner. When carefully trained, however, with their elegant pendulous racemes, their charmingly disposed leaves, their butter yellow autumn foliage, and their sinuous trunks and branches, they are among the most enchanting of all garden plants.

Although the shorter racemed sorts are a success on walls and fences and as shrubs, on the whole the longer racemed cultivars are best on pergolas, around verandahs, over arches or as standards, where the racemes can hang freely and not become entangled with others or with the foliage. If trained against walls these types should be trained with the branches well apart so that this cannot happen. And when grown on pergolas and arches, or as standards, these should be tall enough for people to be able to walk beneath without brushing against the racemes. Under these circumstances they will certainly continue to live up to the lyrical descriptions of Kaempfer, Siebold, Fortune and others in years gone by.

Experience has shown that with W. floribunda careful training and pruning is far more important to ensure floriferousness than it is with W. sinensis and W. brachybotrys. In Japan many growers take tremendous pains in spacing and tying the first, second and third order branches and so on. Kawarada (1985), for instance, gives detailed advice about all this, including instructions for building the traditional Japanese pergola (fujidana) of wood and bamboo and for training the plant over it. I, and I imagine most others elsewhere, have nevertheless been successful with rather more haphazard arrangements.

In Japan they usually prune savagely at the end of flowering (figure 8.1), thinning the plant out somewhat, and then do nothing until autumn, when any untidy shoots are removed. This seems to work quite well there though the plants often are not as floriferous as they are elsewhere. Perhaps this suits Japanese taste. They also remove all the spent racemes, cutting them off just beyond the leafy part, which often produces racemes the next season. I have never been able to bring myself to undertake this mammoth task and, since the seed pods which this species frequently produces are most ornamental (figures 2.1 & 9.1), I leave them until the winter when, if I am feeling energetic, I cut back in the Japanese manner those which have not fallen off of their own accord. They eventually fall off anyway, breaking away just above the last growth bud, though they

can look untidy in late winter and early spring.

What seems to be most important with this species is that any major thinning and reshaping should be done at the end of flowering, and that thereafter all new shoots are shortened back to two or three leaves and not removed completely. This usually involves a major pruning in late spring after the first new growths have appeared, another much less arduous one about six weeks later, followed by a tidying up of the few long shoots produced subsequently so that the plants look neat for the autumn. Having ceased growth they are then particularly attractive when their leaves begin to turn and the pods hang gracefully below. By then they should have a good strong framework with abundant short lateral shoots bearing dormant flower buds.

Flowering as they do on the current year's growth, the American wisterias do not usually display their flowers well if grown on pergolas, though the long-racemed introductions of W. macrostachya may prove to be exceptions in this regard. In general, however, they are seen to best advantage against walls, around verandahs, over fences or as pillars on wooden or metal supports. Under these conditions they may be pruned to keep them within bounds at any time of year. However the extent of my experience with these plants is such that it would be unwise of me to be dogmatic. I suspect, though, that two or three light prunings during the growing season may lead to greater floriferousness than a severe cutting back in autumn or winter. Presumably much the same would apply to the Millettia species described in chapter 7.

Diseases and pests

Wisterias are remarkably free from troublesome diseases and pests, thus preventative treatments and control measures are rarely necessary.

On the whole fungal diseases are of little consequence. When periods of heavy rain coincide with blooming time the flowers sometimes rot, perhaps as a result of infection by a *Botrytis* species. On rare occasions I have noticed this with *W. floribunda,* and others have stated that it particularly affects 'Violacea Plena'. However the condition ceases progression as soon as dry conditions return. There are also scattered records of plants dying as a result of *Armillaria* root-rot, about which nothing practicable can be done, and from time to time fungal leaf spots and powdery mildews cause minor cosmetic damage.

As far as I know there are no records outside Japan of the gall disease of *W. brachybotrys* caused by the bacterium *Erwinia herbicola* pv. *millettiae* mentioned in chapter 5. And virus diseases likewise seem to be of little consequence, although the aphid-borne wisteria vein mosaic virus is occasionally reported to cause a yellow mottling and distortion of the foliage, as is wisteria mosaic virus (Bojnansky & Fargasova 1991). There is no cure, so it is wise to destroy plants should they become infected.

Aphids and scale insects are sometimes observed on wisterias, but rarely in sufficient numbers to warrant control measures. In Australia the flowers may be damaged occasionally by the plague thrips, *Thrips imaginis*. In seasons when these appear they can be controlled by spraying the racemes with insecticides recommended for the purpose, repeating as necessary.

Mites are rarely troublesome except in glasshouses. The red spider or two spotted mite is the species usually encountered under these circumstances and may be controlled by spraying or by biological methods.

In some countries birds have been reported to eat the flower buds and late frosts are known to kill or damage developing racemes. Where this type of frost damage occurs it is usually a prob-

lem only with *W. sinensis*. But since most plants are descended from the original introduction from Guangzhou, this may not be a problem with plants from further north. In particular, in areas where this problem occurs, it would certainly be worth trying plants introduced from Beijing.

Propagation

Wisterias may be raised from seed or propagated by layering, budding, grafting, the removal of suckers and the rooting of cuttings.

The raising of seeds is a very simple matter. They may be planted as soon as ripe, about 2 cm deep in a freely draining mixture, or at any time thereafter. In my experience the seeds exhibit no dormancy. Once temperatures are warm enough, the seeds germinate and the seedlings may be potted on as soon as desired, provided they are kept under mist or shaded and in a humid atmosphere until re-established. Alternatively they may be left until dormant the following winter, then separated and potted individually or planted in rows in the ground.

Since the seed pods burst open violently, flinging the seeds away, the pods should be collected in autumn after leaf fall and allowed to dry in open trays, after which they can easily be broken open by twisting. The short spurs bearing them may be torn off if the pods are pulled from the plant. Hence the rachis should be cut with secateurs immediately beyond the last lateral growth bud, as described in the section on pruning and training.

Of course plants raised from seed will not be identical to their parent or parents, hence the raising of wisterias from seed tends to be discouraged. But while it is sometimes suggested that such plants may take many years to flower, flower poorly, or produce flowers obscured by foliage, such prognostications are unduly discouraging.

Observations of such plants, whether deliberately raised to blooming or originating from grafting stocks which have outgrown the scion, suggest that in most instances the outcome is satisfactory. However, where certainty is required it is best to obtain vegetatively propagated plants. Thus the raising of seedlings is largely carried out in order to provide stock for grafting. Such seedlings are usually raised from *W. floribunda,* as this species sets abundant seeds in most climates.

The vegetative propagation of plants merely involves the making, in one of several ways, of a new plant from a piece of another. Where the parent plant is on its own roots, the simplest method is by the removal of suckers. If the soil around them is loosened, they can be cut or pulled away with roots attached and can then be potted up and left to become established. Late winter is the best time but it can be done in summer, provided they are kept under mist or shaded and in a humid atmosphere until established.

Layering is also a simple procedure. Any long shoot can be used but wisterias often conveniently produce, at the bases of their trunks, long shoots which run along the ground. These shoots readily produce roots along their length if covered with a shallow layer of soil. Once such roots are well developed, a single long shoot can be divided into a number of plants, each of which can be potted as described above.

The rooting of cuttings is a relatively simple matter and is probably the best method for producing plants on their own roots on a commercial scale. No doubt various growers have their preferred technique, and a method which works well for one person under one set of conditions may not prove as successful for others. Thus individuals would be sensible to experiment. It has been noted, for instance, that the rate of success varies according to the time of year the cuttings are taken (Sultan et al. 1990).

In late winter I have used the long unbranched shoots of the previous season, cut into pieces each with three or four buds, their basal ends dipped in 1 per cent indole butyric acid powder. Others use liquid hormone preparations. These are usually used at lower strengths than powders, and experimentation with the strength of the solution and the duration of the dip would seem to be advisable. Also I have been told that keeping cuttings for a period at high temperatures prior to planting out hastens the development of root initials. Such cuttings may be planted directly into the field or in potting mixture in a glasshouse, preferably under conditions where the air temperatures are lower than those of the cutting bed, so that the breaking of the dormancy of the buds is delayed until some roots have developed.

As an amateur I have found the production of roots to be most rapid when cuttings are taken in summer. The greatest success has been achieved using cuttings made from the first crop of new shoots, as soon as the tissues have hardened sufficiently. Each piece may have two or three leaves and, in order for them to be accommodated conveniently in a cutting bed or box, each leaf is shortened to three pairs of leaflets (figure 8.6). Also I have usually removed a shallow slice of bark from the basal 15 mm of one side of the cutting in order to expose additional cambium. As with the dormant cuttings, the basal end of each is dipped in 1 per cent indole butyric acid powder. No doubt liquid preparations could be used instead but I have not tried them. Inserting these cuttings in a mixture of equal parts by volume of peat and perlite has proved to be satisfactory, but no doubt there are other possibilities. Placing each cutting in a 10 cm plastic pot has worked well, as the situation does not arise where the roots are damaged when separating rooted cuttings. Placed under mist with bottom heat of 27–30°C and similar

Figure 8.6 Cutting prepared for insertion

air temperatures, such cuttings usually produce roots in as little as four weeks and can then be hardened off. High temperatures together with the taking of cuttings as early as possible in summer seem to be the secrets of success. Under these conditions the cuttings soon recommence growth and form well-established plants by autumn.

When taking cuttings, as with budding and grafting described below, it is important that the cuts be clean. Plant propagators are often keen on special budding and grafting knives which are regularly sharpened. I have tried these but have found one-sided razor blades to be the most satisfactory for all these procedures, provided they are discarded as soon as they become blunt.

Budding is a relatively simple matter even though under most circumstances it is wiser to use one of the other methods of propagation and produce plants on their own roots. I have found chip budding (figure 8.7a) to be successful when carried out in either late winter or mid-summer. When taking buds in summer the leaves should be cut off carefully as close to the bud as possible. After placing the bud in position it should be tied in and completely covered with plastic

budding tape. When callousing can be seen to have occurred, usually after four to eight weeks, the tape should be removed and the top of the stock plant cut off just above the bud. The bud should then commence growth. All shoots from the stock should be removed as they appear.

In my opinion grafting, like budding, should be avoided unless there is no alternative. In Japan almost all wisterias are grafted onto seedling stock of *W. floribunda*. Large numbers of these plants have found their way round the world and in many cases the stock has outgrown the scion, leaving the resulting plant wrongly labelled with the name of the original scion. This, together with frequent misnaming, has been the cause of much of the present nomenclatural confusion.

Wisterias may be grafted onto vegetatively propagated or seedling stocks or even onto pieces of root taken from established plants. Grafting is best carried out in late winter and various methods may be employed. Where the stock and scion are of the same diameter a whip-and-tongue graft is the neatest (figure 8.7b) but cleft grafting (figure 8.7c) may also be employed. Where the stock is thicker than the scion, a side version of the whip-and-tongue (figure 8.7d) or a cleft graft may be used. When the stock is thicker than the scion it is important, when using a cleft graft, to match the outer sides of stock and scion on one side (figure 8.7e), so that the cambium layers are in contact. The cambium is the layer of cells below the bark that are capable of division and able to bring about the union of stock and scion.

As with budding, once the graft is made it is important to bind it with plastic tape so that the cut surfaces are held tightly together, air is excluded and moisture loss prevented. Alternatively, after tying, the cut surfaces may be sealed with a grafting wax or mastic. Once growth of the scion is well established the ties should be removed. This is particularly important when plastic tape

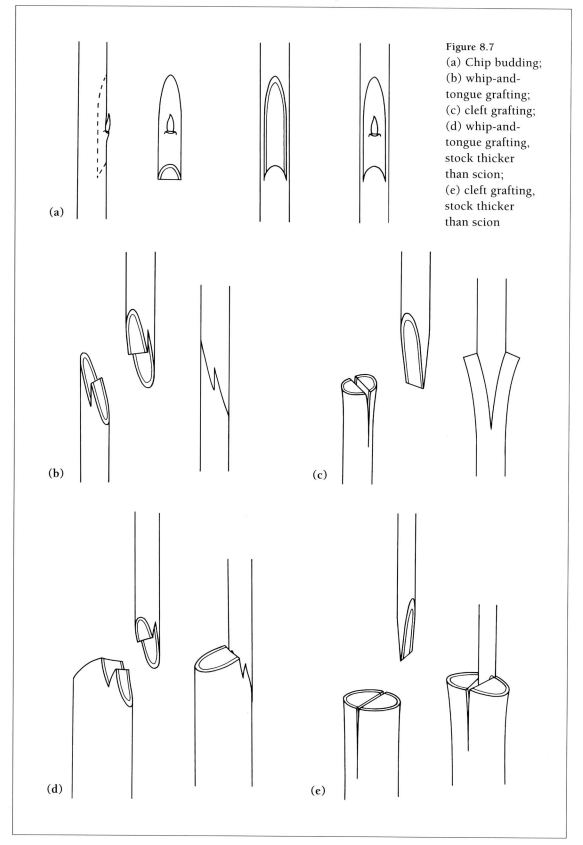

Figure 8.7
(a) Chip budding;
(b) whip-and-
tongue grafting;
(c) cleft grafting;
(d) whip-and-
tongue grafting,
stock thicker
than scion;
(e) cleft grafting,
stock thicker
than scion

has been used, as this does not rot or break easily and may strangle the graft.

The modern technique of micropropagation is undoubtedly the most sophisticated method of vegetative propagation. It involves making a sterile tissue culture under laboratory conditions and keeping it shaken so that the cells separate as they divide. Eventually each cell is treated so that its division results in the formation of a new plant. In this way new varieties, or plants which are otherwise hard to propagate, can be multiplied much more rapidly than could be achieved in any other way. I am unaware of this technique so far being applied to wisterias.

Raising new cultivars

Confronted by this heading, some gardeners will no doubt say, 'Why bother? There is plenty of choice already. We do not wish to be afflicted by a superfluity of cultivars similar to that with which the growers of camellias, rhododendrons, roses and so on have to contend.' While I partly agree with these statements, I can also see that there is, nonetheless, room for improvement. A pure white *W. sinensis* with robust pedicels would be useful, as would a pink one. And another long-racemed white cultivar of *W. floribunda* would be valuable, particularly if it bloomed earlier in the season than 'Shiro Noda'. Perhaps *W. macrostachya* might be used to produce late-blooming hybrids or a programme undertaken to produce cultivars that would enable the cultivation of showy wisterias to extend to colder areas.

The making of deliberate crosses requires patience. For a start, racemes with 100 or more flowers usually set and retain no more than one or two pods, if any at all. Hence it might be necessary to emasculate and pollinate an enormous number of flowers in order to obtain seeds. On the other hand it would be worth trying the removal of all but a few buds from a raceme and then proceeding with the operation. No doubt the problem, if it actually exists, could be overcome under laboratory conditions.

Those intending to breed wisterias should be aware that crosses between species are usually most likely to succeed if the parents have the same chromosome numbers, or at least do not have odd numbers of sets. Thus the information brought together by Bowden (1976) would be of use. It seems that individuals with two sets of eight, a diploid number of sixteen, occur in all the cultivated species. However polyploids (individuals with more than two sets) have been recorded. For instance a triploid, with three sets, has been recorded for *W. floribunda* as has a hexaploid, with six sets. Hexaploids have also been found in *W. frutescens* and *W. macrostachya*.

A possibility which suggests itself is that of producing cultivars with very long racemes by crossing *W. floribunda* 'Macrobotrys', which has 79–128 widely spaced flowers per raceme, with cultivars such as 'Lawrence', which has up to 170 closely spaced flowers per raceme. Similarly it might be possible to produce cultivars with the long racemes of 'Macrobotrys' but with flowers of a deeper colour, or perhaps white or pink.

Within species much could be done simply by surveying them in the wild and introducing superior forms, or by raising large numbers of seedlings and making selections. The raising of seedlings of the white and pink cultivars, for instance, is a project that commends itself.

CHAPTER 9

Recommended Cultivars

To offer advice as to which wisterias are best suited to any particular circumstance is a risky business. Personal preferences concerning colour, scent and form exhibit as much variation as the plants themselves. Also the performance of some of the more recent introductions has not yet been fully assessed, so the following recommendations are likely to be added to in the future. However it is hoped that they will be useful to those looking for guidance.

TOP TEN WISTERIAS

If I were forced to choose only ten wisterias, my choice, not necessarily in order of preference, would be *W. sinensis* 'Consequa', *W. brachybotrys* 'Murasaki Kapitan' and 'Shiro Kapitan' and *W. floribunda* 'Honbeni', 'Kuchibeni', 'Lawrence', 'Macrobotrys', 'Royal Purple', 'Shiro Noda' and 'Violacea Plena'. It may be that, when *W. brachybotrys* 'Okayama' and 'Showa Beni' have been thoroughly tested as garden plants, they will qualify to be added to this list. And I feel a bit guilty about having left out the other cultivars of *W. sinensis*.

Figure 9.1   *Wisteria floribunda* 'Lawrence', seed pods

Figure 9.2 'Formosa' *(left)* and 'Shiro Noda' *(right)* trained as standards

BEST FOR PERGOLAS

Almost any wisteria can look charming on a pergola. However the best effect is created by the long-racemed forms of *W. floribunda*. The old favourite 'Macrobotrys' is impossible to beat under these circumstances. 'Kuchibeni', 'Lawrence', 'Royal Purple' and 'Shiro Noda' are almost as good. I have not seen 'Honbeni' grown this way but I imagine it could be very impressive.

BEST FOR WALLS

Again almost any wisteria can look effective grown in this manner, provided it is trained and pruned so that the branches are spaced taking into account the length of the racemes. This is easier to do with the short-racemed types and it is hard to imagine anything being more successful than *W. sinensis* 'Consequa' or any of the other cultivars of this species and of *W. brachybotrys*. The cultivars of *W. floribunda* tend to be less

showy under these circumstances, though this is not to say that they should be avoided. I have seen many beautiful examples.

BEST AS SHRUBS

Much the same applies here as for walls. On the whole the shorter racemed types look the best. With the long-racemed forms of *W. floribunda* the flowers tend to be obscured by the leaves during the later part of the flowering period.

BEST AS STANDARDS

Almost all of the Asiatic wisterias look wonderful grown as standards (page 6, & figures 1.2 & 9.2). It all becomes a matter of preference regarding time of flowering, colour, scent and so on.

BEST FOR POTS AND BONSAI

Here again it is the short-racemed types that are easiest to handle. The cultivars of *W. sinensis*, *W.*

brachybotrys and those cultivars of *W. floribunda* with 'Issai' as part of their name fulfil these requirements and usually bloom in a relatively short time. However any wisteria can be treated in this manner. For the longer racemed types it is necessary to shape the plant carefully so that the racemes can hang freely.

The variegated cultivars are perhaps most effective grown in pots where the foliage can be admired at close range and any unvariegated shoots noticed and removed as they appear. 'Hime Fuji', the small-leaved dwarf form of *Millettia japonica,* is another plant suited to pot culture.

BEST FOR SCENT

All wisterias are scented. While for many this adds greatly to enjoyment of the flowers, others find it overpowering and they may consider those with the faintest scent to be the best. Many wisterias have a scent described as 'musky', while that of others is said to be 'sweet', so again personal preference plays a role. However by indicating below those cultivars that I have found to have the most pronounced scent, it is hoped that intending growers will be guided in their choice.

The cultivars of *W. brachybotrys* with the strongest scent are 'Murasaki Kapitan' (sweet), 'Okayama' (sweet) and 'Shiro Kapitan' (sweet). For *W. floribunda* my choice would be 'Kuchibeni' (musky), 'Lawrence' (sweet) and 'Royal Purple' (sweet), and for *W. sinensis* 'Amethyst' (sweet) and 'Jako' (musky).

BEST FOR AUTUMN COLOUR

On the whole *W. brachybotrys* and *W. sinensis* and their cultivars are unremarkable in autumn. However the leaves of some young plants of *W. sinensis* raised from seeds collected in China have turned a clear yellow before falling, so there may be exceptions. In the case of *W. brachybotrys* it is only 'Murasaki Kapitan' which exhibits a modest display of this type.

With *W. floribunda* the situation is very different. The leaves of most seedlings and cultivars become yellow before falling. By far the best in this regard is 'Violacea Plena', the bold foliage of which turns a uniform butter yellow (figure 5.36). Almost as good are 'Honbeni', 'Issai Naga', 'Kuchibeni', 'Lawrence', 'Macrobotrys', 'Nagasaki Issai' and 'Royal Purple'.

BEST FOR SEED PODS

If left to develop, the seed pods can be very ornamental and produce a charming effect in summer, autumn and early winter. This is particularly so in *W. floribunda*. Some cultivars set seed more abundantly than others and thus are the more striking. Particularly notable are 'Geisha', 'Lawrence' (figure 9.1), 'Royal Purple' and 'Shiro Noda' which regularly produce heavy crops of long many-seeded pods. Although they produce shorter pods, 'Honbeni', 'Kuchibeni' (figure 5.25) and 'Macrobotrys' (figure 2.1) can also be very ornamental when in fruit.

BEST CULTIVARS BY FLOWER COLOUR

Since there are few cultivars of *W. brachybotrys* and *W. sinensis* from which to choose, there is nothing to be added to the information provided in the appropriate chapters. However with *W. floribunda* there are many choices and the following are recommended: 'Shiro Noda' (white), 'Kuchibeni' (very pale pink), 'Honbeni' (pale pink), 'Lawrence' (pale blue), 'Macrobotrys' (pale violet), 'Royal Purple' (single deep violet) and 'Violacea Plena' (double deep violet).

Glossary

anther: that part of the stamen which produces the pollen.

arbuscule: a finely branched, shrub-like structure produced inside a host cell by a mycorrhizal fungus.

auricle: an ear-like appendage, usually at the base of a leaf or petal.

axil: angle between the upper surface of a leaf or bract and the stem which bears it.

axillary: situated in an axil.

binomial nomenclature: naming by two Latin or Latinised names, the first being the generic name, the second the specific epithet, for example, *Wisteria sinensis*.

bract: leaf-like structure or scale which subtends an inflorescence or flower.

bullate: applied to leaves when the areas between the veins present convexities on one side and concavities on the other; bubble-like.

calyx: outer whorl of flower parts made up of sepals, which are often green and protect the flower in the bud.

cambium: layer of cells which divide to give cells which ultimately form permanent tissue.

claw: narrow base or stalk of a petal.

cotyledon: embryonic first leaf of seed plants.

cultivar: assemblage of cultivated plants, retaining distinguishing features when reproduced.

dextrorse: turning or twisting to the right or clockwise.

diploid: organism having two basic sets of chromosomes, usually one derived from each parent.

emasculate: to remove the anthers from an unopened flower.

embryo: young plant developing from an egg-cell, enclosed within the seed in seed plants.

genus: group of organisms having common characteristics, usually consisting of several species.

glabrous: without hairs.

hypogeal germination: germination where the cotyledons remain below ground, usually within the seed coat.

inflorescence: group of flowers borne on one stem.

keel: structure consisting of the two fused lower petals surrounding the innermost flower parts in pea-flowered legumes.

leaflet: separate portion of a compound leaf.

legume: dry fruit splitting along two longitudinal lines of dehiscence and containing a single row of seeds, for example a pea pod.

mycorrhiza: beneficial symbiotic association between a fungus and the roots of a plant.

ovary: central part of flower which encloses the ovules, and which after fertilisation develops into the fruit.

ovule: structure within the ovary which contains the egg-cell, and which develops into the seed.

panicle: a branched racemose inflorescence.

pedicel: stalk of an individual flower of an inflorescence.

peduncle: stalk of an inflorescence or of a solitary flower.

petal: one of the whorl of flower parts immediately inside the calyx, usually brightly coloured and conspicuous.

petiole: stalk of a leaf.

petiolule: stalk of a leaflet of a compound leaf.

pinnate leaf: compound leaf the leaflets of which are arranged on opposite sides of a common rachis, as in *Wisteria*.

plumule: terminal bud or rudimentary shoot of the embryo of seed plants.

pollen: powdery mass of reproductive bodies produced by the stamens.

polyploid: organism having three or more basic sets of chromosomes.

pubescent: covered with short soft hairs.

raceme: inflorescence of stalked flowers, the youngest at the apex, borne on a simple elongated axis, as in *Wisteria*.

rachis: (1) axis of a pinnate leaf, to which the leaflets are attached; (2) main axis of an inflorescence.

radicle: embryonic root of seed plants.

seed: product of the fertilised ovule, consisting of an embryo, with or without additional food reserves, enclosed within the seed coat.

sepal: one of the parts or lobes of the calyx.

sinistrorse: turning or twisting to the left or anti-clockwise.

species: smallest unit of biological classification commonly used, breeding true within its own limits in nature.

specific epithet: second word of the name of a species which serves to distinguish it from others in the genus, for example, *sinensis*, in the case of *Wisteria sinensis* .

stamen: structure in the flower which produces the pollen, consisting of an anther usually borne on a stalk, the filament.

standard: large petal which stands up at the back of the flower in pea-flowered legumes.

stigma: structure borne by the style adapted for the reception and germination of pollen grains.

style: stalk rising from the ovary, bearing the stigma.

velutinous: velvety.

vesicle: spherical or ellipsoidal swelling of fungal thread.

wing: lateral petal of flower in pea-flowered legumes.

Wisteria brachybotrys 'Showa Beni'

References

Bailey, L. H., et al. 1976. *Hortus Third*. Macmillan, New York.

Bean, W. J. 1980. *Trees and Shrubs Hardy in the British Isles*. 8th edn. John Murray, London.

Bentham, G. 1864. *Flora Australiensis*. Vol. 2, p. 211. Lovell Reeve, London.

Boehmer, L. 1903. 'Wistarias'. *Gardeners' Chronicle* 33(857):347.

Bojnansky, V., and Fargasova, A. 1991. *Dictionary of Plant Virology*. Elsevier, Amsterdam.

Bowden, W. M. 1976. *A Survey of Wisterias in Southern Ontario Gardens*. Technical Bulletin No. 8. Royal Botanical Gardens, Hamilton, Ontario.

Bretschneider, E. 1898. *History of European Botanical Discoveries in China*. Sampson Low, London.

Brickell, C. D., Kelly, A. F., Schneider, F., Voss, E. G., and Richens, R. H. (eds) 1980. *International Code of Nomenclature for Cultivated Plants 1980*. Bohn, Scheltema & Holkema, Utrecht.

Carrière, E.-A. 1878. 'Wistaria sinensis flore pleno'. *Revue Horticole* 1878:260.

Coats, A. 1963. *Garden Shrubs and their Histories*. Vista Books, London.

Cornevin, C. 1893. *Des Plantes Vénéneuses et des Empoisonnements qu'elles Déterminent*. Firmin-Didot, Paris.

De Candolle, A.-P. 1825. *Prodromus*. Vol. 2, p. 390. Treutel and Würtz, Paris.

Dorsett, P. H. 1935. 'Ancient Wistarias of Japan Give Long Flower Racemes'. *Flower Grower* May 1935:212–13.

Du Cane, F. 1908. *The Flowers and Gardens of Japan*. A. & C. Black, London.

Everist, S. L. 1981. *Poisonous Plants of Australia*. Rev. edn. Angus & Robertson, Sydney.

Fernald, M. L. 1950. *Gray's Manual of Botany*, 8th ed. American Book Company, New York.

Forbes, F. B., and Hemsley, W. B. 1887. 'Enumeration of All the Plants Known from China Proper, Formosa, Hainan, Corea, and the Luchu Archipelago, and the Island of Hongkong, together with their Distribution and Synonymy'. *Journal of the Linnean Society. Botany. London* 23:161–62.

Fortune, R. 1847. *Three Years' Wanderings in the Northern Provinces of China*. John Murray, London.

———. 1852. *A Journey to the Tea Countries of China*. John Murray, London.

———. 1863. *Visits to the Capitals of Japan and China*. John Murray, London.

Gardeners' Chronicle. 1925. 'A Giant Wistaria at Wistaria Town'. *Gardeners' Chronicle* 2000:278.

Gardening World. 1904. 'Wisteria multijuga russelliana'. *Gardening World* n.s. 21(14):282. Illustration in supplement.

Geesink, R. 1984. *Scala Millettiearum*. E. J. Brill/Leiden University Press, Leiden.

Gleason, H. A., and Cronquist, A. 1963. *Manual of Vascular Plants of Northeastern United States and Adjacent Canada*. D. Van Nostrand Company, Inc., Princeton, New Jersey.

Greuter et al. (eds). 1988. *International Code of Botanical Nomenclature 1988*. Koeltz Scientific Books, Königstein.

Grootendorst, H. J. 1968. 'Wisteria'. *Dendroflora* 5:61–68.

Guo, S., and Zhou, Z. 1992, in Heerendeen, P. S., and Dilcher, D. L. (eds). *Advances in Legume Systematics*. Part 4, 'The Fossil Record', 207–23. Royal Botanic Gardens, Kew.

Handel-Mazzetti, H. 1921. 'Plantae Novae Sinenses'. *Anzeiger der Akademie der Wissenschaften in Wien. Mathematische-naturwissenschaftliche Klasse* 58(19):177–81.

Hooker, J. D. 1897. 'Wistaria chinensis var. *multijuga*'. *Curtis's Botanical Magazine* 3rd ser. 53:t. 7522.

Houtte, L. van. 1873. 'Wistaria multijuga'. *Flore des Serres et des Jardins d'Europe* 19:125, t. 2002.

Hu, Y. 1988. *Chinese Penjing*. Timber Press, Portland.

Huxley, A., Griffiths, M., and Levy, M. 1992. *The New Royal Horticultural Society Dictionary of Gardening*. Macmillan, London.

Isaacson, R. T. et al. 1989. *Andersen Horticultural Library's Source List of Plants and Seeds*. Andersen Horticultural Library, University of Minnesota, Chanhassen, Minnesota.

Kaempfer, E. 1712. *Amoenitatum Exoticarum*, Fasiculi V, 856–57.

———. 1736. *Histoire et Description Générale du Japon*, Tome Second. J.-M. Gandouin, Paris.

Kaneko, M., Nakata, H., Takada, F., Matsumura, M., Kitagawa, C., Sakashita, S., Nuno, M., and Saito, T. 1988. 'Isoflavones from the Gall and Wood of *Wisteria brachybotrys*'. *Phytochemistry* 27(1):267–69.

Kawarada, S. 1985. *Fuji* ('Wisteria'). NHK Publishing, Tokyo. (In Japanese)

Kingsbury, J. M. 1964. *Poisonous Plants of the United States and Canada*. Prentice Hall, Englewood Cliffs, New Jersey.

Konoshima, T., Kozuka, M., Haruna, M., and Ito, K. 1991. 'Constituents of Leguminous Plants: XIII. New Triterpinoid Saponins from *Wisteria brachybotrys*'. *Journal of Natural Products (Lloydia)* 54(3):830–36.

Konoshima, T., Kozuka, M., Haruna, M., Ito, K., and Kimura, T. 1989. 'Studies on Constituents of Leguminous Plants: XI. The Structures of New Triterpenoids from *Wisteria brachybotrys* Sieb. et Zucc.' *Chemical and Pharmaceutical Bulletin* 37(6):1550–53.

Konoshima, T., Kozuka, M., Haruna, M., Ito, K., Kimura, T., and Tokuda, H. 1989. 'Studies on the Constituents of Leguminous Plants: XII. The Structures of New Triterpinoid Saponins from *Wistaria brachybotrys* Sieb. et Zucc.' *Chemical and Pharmaceutical Bulletin* 37(10):2731–35.

Konoshima, T., Okamoto, E., Kozuka, M., Nishino, H., Tokuda, H., and Tanabe, M. 1988. 'Studies on Inhibitors of Skin Tumor Promotion: III. Inhibitory Effects of Isoflavonoids from *Wisteria brachybotrys* on Epstein-Barr Virus Activation'. *Journal of Natural Products (Lloydia)* 51(6):1266–70.

Krüssman, G. 1962. *Handbuch der Laubgehölze*. Vol. 2, p. 573. Paul Parey, Berlin and Hamburg.

Lancaster, R. 1989. *Travels in China*. Antique Collectors' Club, Woodbridge, Suffolk.

Lavin, M., Doyle, J. J., and Palmer, J. D. 1990. 'Evolutionary Significance of the Loss of the Chloroplast-DNA Inverted Repeat in the Leguminosae Subfamily Papilionoideae'. *Evolution* 44(2):390–402.

Li, H. L. 1959. *The Garden Flowers of China*. Ronald Press, New York.

Lindley, J. 1840. 'Wistaria (or Glycine) Sinensis'. *Edwards's Botanical Register* n.s. 3:41.

———. 1849. 'New Plants, etc., from the Society's Garden: 16. Wistaria Sinensis:*alba*'. *Journal of the Horticultural Society of London* 4:221.

Linnaeus, C. 1753. *Species Plantarum*. Facsimile of 1753 edition with commentary by W. T. Stearn. Ray Society, London, 1957.

Liston, A. 1994. 'Use of the Polymerase Chain Reaction to Survey for the Loss of the Inverted Repeat in the Legume Chloroplast Genome'. In Crisp, M., and Doyle, J. (eds). *Advances in Legume Systematics* 7. Royal Botanic Gardens, Kew.

Louisiana Nursery. 1992. *1992–1993 Catalog of Magnolias and other Garden Aristocrats*. Louisiana Nursery, Opelousas, LA 70570, USA.

McClintock, E. 1973. 'The Generic Name *Wisteria*'. *California Horticultural Journal* 34:159.

McMillan Browse, P. 'Some Notes on Members of the Genus *Wisteria* and their Propagation'. *The Plantsman* 6(2):109–22.

Makino, T, Kikuchi, A., Asami, K., and Namikawa, I. 1955. *Engei Dai-Jiten* ('Horticultural Dictionary'). Seibundo Shinko-sha. (In Japanese)

———. 1970. *Saishin Engei Dai-Jiten* ('New Horticultural Dictionary'). Seibundo Shinko-sha. (In Japanese)

Miyazawa, B. 1940. *Kamoku Engei* ('Cultivation of Trees and Flowers'). Yasaka Shobon. (In Japanese)

Murasaki Shichibu. 10th or 11th century. *The Tale of Genji*. Translated by E. G. Seidensticker. Secker & Warburg, London, 1976.

Nédélec, P.-Y. 1992. 'Gycines'. *L'Ami des Jardins et de la Maison*. Mai 1992:30–37, 128.

Nicholson, G. 1900. *The '1900' Supplement to the Dictionary of Gardening: A Practical and Scientific Encyclopaedia of Horticulture for Gardeners and Botanists*. Upcott Gill, London.

Norimura, H., Hirashiki, I., Ogata, F., Yoshida, N., and Ito, A. 1990. 'Purification of Bowman-Birk Type Inhibitor of High Molecular Weight from Wisteria Seeds'. *Agricultural and Biological Chemistry* 54(11):3029–30.

Nuttall, T. 1818. *The Genera of North American Plants II*. Printed for the author by D. Heartt, Philadelphia.

Oehme, F. W. 1978, in Keeler, R. F., et al. (eds). *Effects of Poisonous Plants on Livestock*. Academic Press, New York.

Ohwi, J. 1965. *Flora of Japan*. Smithsonian Institute, Washington, DC.

Phillipi, D. L. (translator). 1969. *Kojiki*. Princeton University Press and Tokyo University Press.

Planchon, J. E. 1853. '*Wisteria brachybotrys* Sieb. et Zucc.' *Flore des Serres et des Jardins d'Europe* 9:61, t. 880.

Poiret, J. 1823, in Lamarck, *Encycopédie Méthodique: Botanique,* vol. 3. p. 674. V. Agasse, Paris.

Prain, D. (ed.). 1919. 'Wisteria venusta'. *Curtis's Botanical Magazine* 4th ser. 25:t. 8811.

Rehder, A. 1922. 'New Species, Varieties and Combinations from the Herbarium and Collections of the Arnold Arboretum'. *Journal of the Arnold Arboretum* 3:12–50.

———. 1926a. 'New Species, Varieties and Combinations from the Herbarium and Collection of the Arnold Arboretum'. *Journal of the Arnold Arboretum* 7:149.

———. 1926b. 'Enumeration of the Ligneous Plants of Northern China: III'. *Journal of the Arnold Arboretum* 7:151–227.

———. 1927. *Manual of Cultivated Trees and Shrubs Hardy in North America.* Macmillan, New York.

———. 1949. *Bibliography of Cultivated Trees and Shrubs Hardy in the Cooler Temperate Regions of the Northern Hemisphere.* Arnold Arboretum of Harvard University, Massachusetts.

——— and Wilson, E. H. 1916. 'Wistaria'. In C. S. Sargent (ed.). *Plantae Wilsonianae,* vol. 2, pp. 509–15. Arnold Arboretum Publication No. 4, Harvard University Press, Cambridge, Massachusetts.

Robinson, B. J., and Fernald, M. L. 1908. *Gray's New Manual of Botany.* 7th edn. American Book Company, New York.

Sabine, J. 1826. 'On *Gycine Sinensis*'. *Transactions of the Horticultural Society of London* 6:460–64.

Schot, A. M. 1994. 'A Revision of *Callerya* Endl. (incl. *Padbruggea* Miq. and *Whitfordiodendron* Elm.) (Papilionaceae: Millettieae)'. *Blumea* 39:1–40.

Siebold, P. F. von, and Zuccarini, J. G. 1835–41. *Flora Japonica.* Vol. 1, pp. 88–93. Lugduni Batavorum.

Sims, J. 1819. 'Glycine sinensis'. *Curtis's Botanical Magazine* 46:t. 2083.

Sirén, O. 1949. *Gardens of China.* Ronald Press, New York.

Sitwell, O. 1935. *Penny Foolish.* Macmillan, London.

Spae, D. 1847. '*Wisteria brachybotrys* Zucc. et Sieb.' *Annales de la Societé Royale d'Agriculture et de Botanique de Gand* 3:49–50, t.

Stackhouse, J. 1981. *Mr. Macleay's Garden.* Compiled for an exhibition at Elizabeth Bay House, June–August 1981. Historic Houses Trust of NSW, Sydney.

Stegermark, J. A. 1963. *Flora of Missouri.* Iowa State University Press, Ames, Iowa.

Stritch, L. R. 1984. 'Nomenclatural Contribution to a Revision of the Genus *Wisteria*'. *Phytologia* 56:183–84.

Suga, T. 1991. *The Man'yo-shu: A Complete Translation in 5–7 Rhythm.* Kanda Institute of Foreign Languages.

Sultan, S. M., Saleem, M. D., and Al-Atrakchii, A. O. 1990. 'Propagation of *Wisteria floribunda* D.C. by Hardwood Cuttings'. *Mesopotamia Journal of Agriculture* 22(4):53–62.

Thunberg, C. P. 1784. *Flora Japonica.* Lipsiae Mülleriano.

Torrey, J., and Gray, A. 1838. *A Flora of North America.* Vol. 1, p. 283. Hafner, New York (reprinted 1969).

Tsukamoto, Y. 1984. *Kaben Engei Dai-Jiten* ('Dictionary of Flowers in Colour'). Yokendo, Tokyo. (In Japanese)

Uehara, K. 1961. *Jumoku Dai-Zusetsu* ('Illustrated Dictionary of Trees'). Ariake Shobo. (In Japanese)

Usher, G. 1974. *A Dictionary of Plants Used by Man.* Constable, London.

Voss, E. G. 1985. *Michigan Flora.* Cranbrook Institute of Science Bulletin 59 and University of Michigan Herbarium, Ann Arbor.

Ward, C. 1912. *Royal Gardens.* Longmans Green & Company, London.

Watanabe, I., Yanai, T., Awano, K., Kogami, K., and Hayashi, K. 1988. 'Volatile Components of *Wisteria* Flower'. *Developments in Food Science* 18:425–37.

Willdenow, C. L. von. 1802. 'Glycine floribunda'. In Linnaeus, C., *Species Plantarum,* 4th edn, p. 1066, no. 40. Nauk, Berlin.

Wilson, E. H. 1913. *A Naturalist in Western China,* vol. 1, p. 18. Methuen, London.

———. 1916. 'The Wistarias of China and Japan'. *Gardeners' Chronicle* 1545:61–62.

Wohlert, A. E. 1937. *Oriental Wistarias.* Garden Nurseries, Penn Valley, Narbeth, Pennsylvania.

Wyman, D. 1949. 'The Wisterias'. *Arnoldia* (Jamaica Plain) 9(5–6):17–28.

———. 1961. 'Showy Wisteria Still a Problem Vine'. *American Nurseryman* 113(11):10–11, 68–76.

———. 1969. *Shrubs and Vines for American Gardens.* Rev. edn. Macmillan, New York.

Index